SEPHER HA-RAZIM

Society of Biblical Literature

TEXTS AND TRANSLATIONS
PSEUDEPIGRAPHA SERIES

Harold W. Attridge, Editor

Texts and Translations 25
Pseudepigrapha Series 11

SEPHER HA-RAZIM
The Book of the Mysteries

Translated by
Michael A. Morgan

SEPHER HA-RAZIM
The Book of the Mysteries

Translated by
Michael A. Morgan

Scholars Press
Chico, California

SEPHER HA-RAZIM
The Book of the Mysteries

Translated by
Michael A. Morgan

Library of Congress Cataloging in Publication Data
Sepher ha-razim. English.
  Sepher ha-razim: The book of the mysteries.

  (Pseudepigrapha series ; 11) (Texts and transla-
tions ; 25)
  Translation of: Sefer ha-razim.
1. Cabala. I. Morgan, Michael A. II. Title. III. Title:
Book of the mysteries. IV. Series. V. Series: Texts and
translations ; 25.
BM525.A3712M67   1983   296.1'6   82-25181
ISBN 0-89130-615-3

Printed in the United States of America

TEXTS AND TRANSLATIONS is a project of the Committee on
Research and Publications of the Society of Biblical Literature and
is under the general direction of Kent H. Richards (Iliff School of
Theology), Executive Secretary, and Leander Keck (Yale Divinity
School), Chairman of the Committee. The purpose of the project is
to make available in convenient and inexpensive format ancient texts
which are not easily accessible but are of importance to scholars and
students of "biblical literature" as broadly defined by the Society.
Reliable modern English translations will accompany the texts. The
following subseries have been established thus far:

PSEUDEPIGRAPHA, edited by

Harold W. Attridge (Southern Methodist University)

GRECO-ROMAN RELIGION, edited by

Hans Dieter Betz (University of Chicago)

Edward N. O'Neil (University of Southern California)

EARLY CHRISTIAN LITERATURE, edited by

Robert L. Wilken (University of Notre Dame)

William R. Schoedel (University of Illinois)

For the PSEUDEPIGRAPHA SERIES the choice of texts is governed
in part by the research interests of the SBL Pseudepigrapha Group,
of which John J. Collins (De Paul University) is currently Chairman,
and James H. Charlesworth (Duke University) is Secretary. This
series will focus on Jewish materials from the Hellenistic and
Greco-Roman periods and will regularly include the fragmentary
evidence of works attributed to biblical personalities, culled from

a wide range of Jewish and Christian sources. The volumes are
selected, prepared, and edited in consultation with the following
editorial committee of the Pseudepigrapha Group: Sebastian P.
Brock (Cambridge University, England), Robert A. Kraft (University
of Pennsylvania), George W. MacRae (Harvard Divinity School), George
W. E. Nickelsburg, Jr. (University of Iowa), Michael E. Stone
(Hebrew University, Israel), and John Strugnell (Harvard Divinity
School).

 In the current volume the series presents only an English
translation of an ancient text. This divergence from the usual
practice is due to the fact that the Hebrew text of the Sepher
Ha-Razim is readily available in a recent edition, while no English
translation exists. It is hoped that the current volume will make
more widely known this important work of Jewish magical literature.

         Harold W. Attridge, Editor

FOREWORD

I wish to express my appreciation to the University of Alberta
for the research grant which made the work on this text possible and
to Joan Paton, Rhoda Zuk, and Gerane West who assisted in the
preparation of the manuscript. Helpful suggestions concerning
translation and understanding were received from Harold W. Attridge,
Theodore H. Gaster and Roy David Kotansky. Their ideas and
suggestions have been incorporated into the text. Most of all I
would like to thank Morton Smith, who undertook a detailed review
of the translation and whose knowledge and insight made it possible.

                                        Michael A. Morgan

TABLE OF CONTENTS

Series Preface   v

Foreword   vii

Introduction   1

Sigla   14

Sepher Ha-Razim, Translation   15

    First Firmament   21
    Second Firmament   43
    Third Firmament   61
    Fourth Firmament   67
    Fifth Firmament   73
    Sixth Firmament   77
    Seventh Firmament   81

Appendix: Angelic Lists   87

Indices   91

INTRODUCTION

In 1963, while studying Kabbalistic texts at Oxford, Mordecai
Margalioth happened upon a Genizah fragment which gave a magical
praxis to assist one in winning at the racetrack. Recalling similar
formulas from the Genizah collection and elsewhere, he began a
detailed study of the preserved fragments of magical literature. He
postulated that these fragments may have all come from a common
source which could be reconstructed. His research led to the
publication of Sepher Ha-Razim in 1966.

The published text is eclectic. No single document available
to Margalioth contained all of the material which was to appear in
the final text. Enough was available, however, that he felt
confident that he had successfully reconstructed a magical handbook
from the early Talmudic period. Since its publication, SHR has
proven a valuable source of information for studies pertaining to
magic in antiquity and for studies relating to Jewish life in the
first centuries CE.

Margalioth was an excellent textual scholar. Even though
additional texts have come to light since the publication of SHR,
his original work is an exceptional piece of scholarship which
demands wider circulation and use among scholars interested in the
Judaisms of the Hellenistic age. No doubt a re-editing of SHR is
needed in the future. For the present, I hope the scholarly
community will find this annotated translation of the Margalioth
text a valuable tool for further study.

1

A. THE MANUSCRIPTS

<u>Codices</u>

There were seven major codices available to Margalioth for the
preparation of his text. Each of them contained significant portions
of what was to become SHR.

1. ק - The Kaufman manuscript in the Oriental Library of the
   Hungarian Academy in Budapest. No. 224, pp. 41-63.

2. א - Jewish Theological Seminary Manuscript Library,
   JTSL no. 163, p. 15A to p. 48B.

3. ב - Jewish Theological Seminary Manuscript Library,
   JTSL no. N.014, p. 8B to p. 28B.

4. פ - The Florence Manuscript in the Library Medicea
   Laurenziana, no. Plut. 44.13, p. 107B to p. 118A.

5.   A manuscript in the National Library, Jerusalem,
     Heb. 8° 476, p. 69B to p. 81B.

6.   Schocken Manuscript, Schocken Library, Jerusalem,
     Kabbalah Manuscript 3. This is a copy of the
     Florence manuscript.

7. ס - Jewish Theological Seminary Manuscript Library,
   JTSL no. N.012, pp. 1-24.

Of these seven manuscripts Margalioth used only the five marked with
Hebrew letter designations. All of the first six are arranged
similarly and are bound together with <u>Maseket Hekhaloth</u>, <u>Maaseh
Bereshit</u>, and <u>Shiur Komah</u>. They all contain similar omissions, both
accidental and deliberate, by the scribes. Ms. 1 (ק) seems to be
the superior version, often completing words and sentences which are
omitted in the other versions. It is the most precise and appears
to contain the fewest distortions. Mss. 5 and 6 contained no
material of special significance and were not used. Ms. 7 (ס) is an
expanded and elaborated version. Its editor states that it was
produced from two documents, a shorter Hebrew text and an expanded

Latin translation. The lists of angelic names in this version are

more extensive than in the others. The text alternates languages

and gives both versions in places. In addition, Margalioth (Sepher,

50-51) lists four manuscripts which were not available to him.

Hebrew Genizah Fragments

The following fragments are designated א.

1. Oxford MS. Heb. C. 18/30:
   One parchment page containing nineteen lines on each
   side. The beginning letters of each line on side one and
   the concluding letters of each line on side two--from the
   middle of the page to the bottom--are mutilated.
   Content: The beginning of SHR to 1:6.

4. Cambridge T-S K 1/97:
   One small paper page containing twenty lines on both
   sides. Content: 1:13-54.

10. Cambridge T-S K 1/145:
    Two large paper pages which are mutilated on all four
    sides, partially illegible, and torn. The remainder
    has thirty-six/thirty-seven lines per side.
    Content: 2:100-4:47.

14. Cambridge T-S K 21/95, fragment 2:
    One small paper page containing twenty lines on side one
    only. Content: 7:1-9.

The following fragments are designated 1א.

2. Adler JTSL ENA 2750, pp. 4-5.
   Two small pages containing seventeen lines on each
   side--torn and often illegible. Content: P:1-1:1.

6. Cambridge T-S N.S. 135:
   One page containing twenty-one lines on each side--torn
   and often illegible. Content: 1:47-71.

11. Cambridge T-S K 1/102:
    One page containing twenty-one lines on each side.
    Content: 3:15-46.

12. Cambridge T-S K 1/13:
    One page containing twenty lines on side one and
    seventeen lines on side two. Content: 4:8-30.

The following fragments are designated 2λ.

> 3. Cambridge T-S K 21/95:
>   One parchment page containing twenty-two lines on side one
>   and twenty-four lines on side two. Content: P:10-1:18.
>   Similar to 1λ #1.

> 13. Cambridge T-S N.S. 246/26:
>   One page containing sixteen-seventeen lines per side
>   but some lines are missing from the top of the page.
>   Content: 4:29-52.

The following fragments are designated ב.

> 5. Cambridge T-S K 1/98:
>   One parchment page containing twenty-six lines on each
>   side. The beginning lines on side one and the concluding
>   lines on side two are mutilated. Content: 1:17/65.

> 7. Oxford MS. Heb. D. 62/50:
>   One page mutilated diagonally from the top of the page
>   through line 5. Side two is illegible. Content: 2:30-76.

> 9. Leningrad Antonine Collection No. 238:
>   One parchment page. Content: 2:30-76.

The following fragment received no designation:

> 8. Adler JTSL ENA 2673/23.
>   One paper page, badly mutilated. Content: 1:237-2:25.

The Arabic Fragments

There are ten arabic fragments which were found by Margalioth in
the Genizah material. They are designated ע or 1ע where they are
duplicates.

> 1. Oxford MS. Heb. f.45:
>   Eighteen parchment pages and by far the most important
>   of the Arabic Fragments. Content: 1:6-2:8.

> 2. Oxford MS. Heb. e. 67/32-33:
>   Two pages. Content: 1:1-18.

> 3. Cambridge T-S Arabic 31/183:
>   One page. Content: 1:1-100.

> 4. Cambridge T-S Arabic 43/260.

5. Cambridge T-S N.S. 298/72:
   Two pages torn at the top and missing some sections in
   the middle. Begins with 2:204.

6. Cambridge T-S Arabic 43/84:
   Two pages. Page one begins with 2:130 and page two begins
   with 4:10.

7. Dropsie College, Philadelphia, Genizah Collection no. 437.
   One very torn parchment page. Begins with 4:10.

8. Cambridge T-S Arabic 45/12:
   One page beginning at 3:51, and then omitting the fourth
   firmament and continuing with the fifth firmament.

9. Cambridge T-S Arabic 33/9:
   One parchment page beginning with the last line of the
   third firmament (3:58) and continuing with the fifth
   firmament.

10. Cambridge T-S Arabic 43/223:
    One page beginning with 4:38.

Latin Translation

The Latin translation is titled <u>Liber Razielis Angeli</u> and is
found in the Senate Library in Leipzig, Codex Latinus No. 745.
Margalioth did not receive a copy of this manuscript until after the
type had been set for the Hebrew edition. Consequently he refers to
only a few places in it. Unlike the Arabic, the Latin is a free
translation and adaptation which has been greatly expanded. Of the
Hebrew codices, it is closest to ס, whose editor claims to have used
a Latin version.

Other Sources

Margalioth drew heavily upon many medieval collections of
magical spells and formulas which he felt were descended from his
postulated original. The most important of these are:

1. <u>Sepher Raziel</u>, Amsterdam 1701.   Siglum: ר.

2. <u>Sepher Raziel</u>, manuscripts and fragments. cf. Margalioth,
   <u>Sepher</u>, 44f.

3. Sepher Kamay ^cot, JTSL 2272. Siglum: ח.

4. Sepher Kamay ^cot, fragments. cf. Margalioth, Sepher, 51.

5. Mafteach Shlomo, Facsimile Oxford 1914. Siglum: ח.

6. Sepher Ha-Malbush, Kaufman 245. Siglum: ל.

A visual representation of the eclectic nature of the text can be
found on the chart produced by Niggemeyer, Beschwörungsformeln,
between pages 18 and 19.

B. STRUCTURE

The text of SHR is divided into seven unequal sections
preceeded by a preface which contains a description of the book's
transmission and functions. Before the flood, it was presented by
the angel.Raziel to Noah who used it as a guide. After the flood it
was passed down through the Biblical generations to Solomon.

The structure of the seven heavens reflects the fairly common
cosmology known from Jewish circles during the Hellenistic age. It
has close parallels to Talmudic passages, the Enoch literature, and
the Hekhaloth literature. The heavens are divided as follows:

1.   The first firmament has seven separate encampments. Each
     encampment is ruled by an angelic overseer who has
     numerous angels listed as serving him.

2.   The second firmament is divided into twelve steps or
     levels. Each has between nine and twenty angels who can
     be called upon.

3.   The third firmament is ruled by three angels. Each has a
     troop of angels which serve him.

4.   The fourth firmament is divided between thirty-one angelic
     princes and their encampments who lead the sun during the
     day and thirty-one angelic princes and their encampments
     who lead the sun during the night.

5.   The fifth firmament is ruled by twelve princes of glory
     who represent the twelve months of the year.

6.   The sixth firmament is divided between an eastern overlord
     who rules twenty-eight angelic leaders and their
     encampments and a western overlord who rules thirty-one
     angelic leaders and their encampments.

7.   The seventh firmament is a description of the divine throne
     followed by a long doxology.

Each firmament, except the seventh, and each subdivision is
described as to its nature and function. For each subdivision there
is a magical praxis described which can be initiated by calling upon
the angels listed in that subdivision and by following the prescribed
rites. With few exceptions, the magical praxis will reflect the
descriptions of either the angels or the heaven itself. The rules of
sympathy and contagion are clearly in evidence.

With minor exceptions, this is an outline of the over all
structure of any given subdivision.

I. A description of the firmament followed by

    A. A description of the subdivision and its usage
       organized thus:

       1. Names of the angels of the subdivision

       2. Description of the angels and their function

       3. The purpose these angels can be made to serve

       4. The procedures to be followed in preparation

       5. The invocation to be spoken to initiate the
          praxis (in some cases this has been lost)

       6. In some cases, additional actions and/or
          invocations to assist, alter, or reverse
          the magical praxis

A fine analysis of the form and style of these incantations and
invocations has been done by Niggemeyer, Beschwörungsformeln, 63-118.

C. DATE

Dating an eclectic text is difficult at best. The consensus of
those scholars who have worked with the text is to support Margalioth's dating of SHR to the early fourth or late third century CE.[1]
The reasons generally listed for this are:

1.   The reference to the Roman indictions in 1:27-28 (cf.
      Margalioth, Sepher, 24) gives a clear terminus a quo of
      297 CE.

2.   The majority of the text is written in a pure midrashic
      Hebrew which reflects the period.

3.   Many of the Greek words found in the text are technical
      terms used in the magical praxeis of that period.

4.   The spells and incantations of SHR closely parallel the
      magical material preserved in the Greek magical papyri and
      in the Aramaic incantation bowls.

5.   The forms of the adjurations are similar to material we
      know from the early Rabbinic literature.

6.   The cosmological framework of the text reflects the Enoch
      and Hekhaloth literature of that period.

Although Margalioth's basic assumptions have gained the support of
the majority of scholars, we must understand exactly what it is we
are dating.

There are two different types of document here. The first is a
cosmological framework which shows a marked similarity with the
hekhaloth literature. The second is a collection of unrelated
magical praxeis which show a marked similarity to the materials
preserved in PGM. Chen Merchavya (JE 13, 1594-95) implies that the
praxeis were woven into the descriptions of the angels and the

---

[1]A notable exception to the consensus is Ithamar Gruenwald,
(Apocalyptic, 226), who dates the work to sixth or seventh century.

heavens. This would make the cosmological framework the primary
document. Surely the reverse is true. Gruenwald points out the SHR
should not be classed as hekhalot literature despite its similarity.
The magical praxeis are the primary source.

It seems to me more likely that the magical praxeis have been
provided with a cosmological framework intended to make them appear
as legitimate Jewish practices. Thus the formulas, spells, and
incantations presumably existed prior to their present form. The
use of Greek and Aramaic words is limited to the actual praxeis.
The language of those sections is simple and straightforward. It
lacks the flowery descriptive wording and the Biblical quotations of
the cosmological framework. The only exception to this lies in the
long adjurations of the latter firmaments and these hardly seem part
of the original praxeis themselves. SHR has a cosmology which
concerns itself in great detail with Jewish ritual purity, but
praxeis which demand we eat cakes made from blood and flour. We
have a framework which speaks of the glory of YHWH, but praxeis
which offer prayers to Helios, and invoke Hermes and Aphrodite. We
should indeed date SHR to the early fourth century CE but it is
crucial to recognize that what fascinates us most about this text,
the magic, is part of a folk tradition which dates from an earlier
time. For example, the idol used to quell a rising river in
2:115ff. is clearly one which the Rabbis in Avodah Zarah 3:1 forbid
Jews to make or possess. Since the Rabbis found it necessary to ban
the image, one must assume that it was in popular use prior to the
Mishnah's compilation. In dating SHR we are not dating the
antiquity of the praxeis themselves.

Just as we cannot date an eclectic text by reference to any one
section, so we cannot determine its origin by any one section. Even
a number of references will afford no more than a list of possibilities. It is far too easy to be led to a conclusion, for example,
that SHR is of Egyptian-Jewish origin. The oldest fragments were
preserved there. The passage of the sun to the East via the North
reflects Egyptian mythology. The use of hieratic papyrus was a sign
of the Egyptian priesthood's magical rites. The listing of the
descent through the mother was a common Egyptian practice and of
course the Roman indictions point to a possible Alexandrian origin.
Most compelling, however, is the close similarity between the
material preserved in SHR and that of PGM.

Such a listing is persuasive until objectively analyzed. That
an Egyptian Jewish scribal community preserved the text is no
argument for its authorship. The sun's passage is part of other
folklores and was surely a common theme in the ancient world.
Hieratic papyrus was known as a magical tool outside of Egypt.
Descent through the mother was a popular aphorism of the Greco-Roman
world as well as a basis for Jewish legal definitions and serves in
SHR to insure the effectiveness of the praxis. The indictions were
used throughout the Roman world and could easily have been part of a
document written in Constantinople. That there are close similarities between SHR and PGM is surely of interest but close similarities
also exist between SHR and the incantation bowls of Syria. Furthermore, that PGM was found only in Egypt merely points out how
fortunate we are that Egypt's climate is so well suited for
preserving such material.

Magic was the common property of the people of the Greco-Roman
world. The praxeis could have arisen in any part of that world and
have been initially preserved in any part of that world. To attempt
to locate a single place of origin would be futile.

Furthermore, we should not attempt to place the magical praxeis
of SHR within any specific group. The praxeis are part of the
popular religion of the age. Jews who could place a mosaic of
Helios on their synagogue floors certainly could not have found it
strange to offer invocations to that same god. On the other hand,
SHR has clearly undergone editing at the hands of more "tradition-
ally" or rabbinically oriented scribes. We can sense the tensions
between a developing orthodoxy and a popular religion here. SHR
is a fine example of the syncretistic nature of the Hellenistic
world.

D. THE TRANSLATION

A translation either can be literal, to render the exact words
of the Hebrew, or can be paraphrastic to catch the meaning. This
translation contains elements of both sorts. Its purpose is to
convey the meaning in each case as clearly as possible. Parentheses
have been used to set off words and phrases which are not found in
the Hebrew text, but are either implied, understood, or needed to
create a readable translation.

I have attempted to follow the Margalioth text as closely as
possible. When a different reading is offered it is so footnoted.
The technical Greek terms and prayers have been translated in the
text and footnoted.

The angelic lists presented a special problem. There was so much conjecture involved in creating these lists in transliterated form that I opted, for the sake of consistency and accuracy, to produce the lists without the speculative vocalization. For those who find this an unsatisfactory solution, I have provided the Hebrew lists in Appendix I.

Hebrew/English equivalents for the text are as follows:

' =	א	L =	ל
B =	ב	M =	מ
G =	ג	N =	נ
D =	ד	S =	ס
H =	ה	ᶜ =	ע
W =	ו	P =	פ
Z =	ז	Ṣ =	צ
Ḥ =	ח	Q =	ק
Ṭ =	ט	R =	ר
Y =	י	Ṡ =	שׁ
K =	כ	T =	ת

E. ABBREVIATIONS AND SHORT TITLES

DMP	Francis L. Grifith, The Demotic Magical Papyrus, London: H. Grevel & Co., 1904.
Ginzberg, Legends	Louis Ginzberg, Legends of the Jews, Philadelphia: Jewish Publication Society, 1937.
Goodenough, Symbols	Erwin R. Goodenough, Jewish Symbols in the Greco-Roman Period, New York: Pantheon Books, 1953-1968.
Gruenwald, Apocalyptic	Ithamar Gruenwald, Apocalyptic and Merkavah Mysticism, Leiden: E. J. Brill, 1980.
Jastrow, Dictionary	Marcus Jastrow, A Dictionary of the Targumim The Talmud Babli and Yerushalmi and the Midrashic Literature, New York: The Judaica Press, 1971.
JE	Jewish Encyclopaedia, Jerusalem: Keter Publishing Ltd., 1972.
Margalioth, Sepher	Mordecai Margalioth, Sepher Ha-Razim, Jerusalem: Yediot Achronot, 1966.
Niggemeyer, Beschwörungsformeln	J. H. Niggemeyer, Beschwörungsformeln aus dem Buch der Geheimnisse, Hildersheim: Georg Olms Verlag, 1975.
PGM	Karl Preisendanz, Papyri Graecae Magicae, Leipzig: B. G. Teubner, vol. I 1928, vol. II 1931. Quoted by papyrus and line number.
SHR	Sepher Ha-Razim

SIGLA

א   JTSL no. 163. See p. 2.

ב   JTSL no. N. 014. See p. 2.

ג   Geniza fragments. See pp. 3-4.

ד   Sepher Raziel. See p. 5.

ה   Sepher Kamay^cot. See p. 6.

ח   Mafteach Shlomo. See p. 6.

ל   Sepher Ha-Malbush. See p. 6.

נ   Geniza fragments. See p. 4.

ס   JTSL no. N. 012. See p. 2.

ע   Arabic fragments. See p. 4.

פ   Florence MS Laurenziana, no Plut. 44.13. See p. 2.

ק   Kaufman. MS. See p.2.

SEPHER HA-RAZIM

TRANSLATION

(PREFACE)

This is a book, from the Books of the Mysteries, which was given to Noah, the son of Lamech, the son of Methuselah, the son of Enoch, the son of Jared, the son of Mehallalel, the son of Kenan, the son of Enosh, the son of Seth, the son of Adam, by Raziel the angel in the year[1] when he came into the ark (but) before his entrance.

And (Noah) inscribed it upon a sapphire stone[2] very distinctly.[3] And he learned from it how to do wondrous deeds, and (he learned) secrets of knowledge, and categories of

5 understanding and thoughts of humility and concepts of counsel, (how) to master the investigation of the strata of the heavens, to go about in all that is in their seven abodes, to observe all the astrological signs, to examine the course of the sun, to explain the observations of the moon, and to know the paths of the Great Bear, Orion, and the Pleiades,[4] to declare the names of the overseers of each and every firmament and the realms of their authority, and by what means they (can be made to) cause success in each thing (asked of them), and what are the names of their attendants and what (oblations) are to be

---

[1]Ms. א reads בשעה but "hour" is probably incorrect, as "hour" could be taken to imply the exact moment and to contradict the sense of לפני .

[2]Cf. Ginzberg, Legends, 1.157, 5.179.

[3]Cf. Deut 27:8

[4]Cf. Job 9:9; Amos 5:8.

poured out to them, and what is the proper time (at which they

10   will hear prayer,[5] so as) to perform every wish of anyone

(who comes) near them in purity. (Noah learned) from it

rituals (that cause) death and rituals (that preserve) life, to

understand the evil and the good, to search out (the right)

seasons and moments (for magical rites), to know the time to

give birth and the time to die, the time to strike and the time

to heal,[6] to interpret dreams and visions, to arouse combat,

and to quiet wars, and to rule over spirits and over demons, to

send them (wherever you wish) so they will go out like slaves,[7]

15   to watch the four winds of the earth, to be learned in the

speech of thunderclaps, to tell the significance of lightning

flashes, to foretell what will happen in each and every month,

and to know the affairs of each and every year, whether for

plenty or for hunger, whether for harvest or for draught,

whether for peace or for war, to be as one of the awesome ones

and to comprehend the songs of heaven.

And from the wisdom of the secrets of this book, Noah

learned and understood how to make gopher wood (into) an ark

20   and to hide from the torrent of the flood waters, to bring (the

animals) with him two by two and seven by seven, to take in

some of every kind of food and every kind of provender. And he

placed (the book) in a golden cabinet and brought it first into

---

[5] Literally "it (prayer) will be heard by them."

[6] Cf. Eccl 3:2,3.

[7] Cf. Job 38:35.

the ark, to learn from it the times of the day and to

investigate from it the times of the night, and in which period

he should arise to pour out entreaties. And when he came forth

from the ark, he used (the book) all the days of his life, and

at the time of his death he handed it down to Abraham,[8] and

Abraham to Isaac, and Isaac to Jacob, and Jacob to Levi, and

25   Levi to Kohath, and Kohath to Amram, and Amram to Moses, and

Moses to Joshua, and Joshua to the elders, and the elders to

the prophets, and the prophets to the sages,[9] and thus genera-

tion by generation until Solomon the King arose. And the Books

of the Mysteries were disclosed to him and he became very

learned in books of understanding, and (so) ruled over every-

thing he desired, over all the spirits and the demons that

wander in the world, and from the wisdom of this book he

imprisoned and released, and sent out and brought in, and built

and prospered.[10] For many books were handed down to him, but

this one was found more precious and more honorable and more

30   difficult than any of them. Happy the eye that will behold

---

[8]Mss. ס and ז insert Shem into the chronology.

[9]Cf. Pirke Avoth 1:1. This genealogy is similar to the Avot
tradition but it puts Solomon the King after the prophets and
the sages. Since they should follow Solomon, it seems that an
original genealogy ending with Solomon (probably after "elders")
has been interpolated by an editor who wanted to claim knowledge of these secrets for the rabbis. Evidence for such an
insertion is important because it casts some doubt on other
Rabbinic elements in the text, and because of the fact that a
Rabbinic editor left the pagan elements stand, illustrates an
unfamiliar side of Rabbinic Judaism.

[10]Cf. Ginzberg, Legends, 4.149-154, 165-169; Josephus,
Antiquities, 8.2.5, #45-49.

it. Happy the ear that listens attentively to its wisdom.

For in it are the seven firmaments and all that is in them.

From their encampments we shall learn to comprehend all things,

and to have success in every deed, to think and to act from the

wisdom of this book.

(THE FIRST FIRMAMENT)

The name of the first firmament is called *Shamayim*.[1]
Within it are encampments filled with wrath. And seven thrones
are prepared there and upon them are seated overseers, and
around them on all sides encampments (of angels) are stationed
and are obedient to men at the time when they practice (magic),
to everyone who has learned to stand and pour (libations) to
their names and cite them by their signs[2] at the period when
5   (prayer) is heard (so as) to make a magical rite succeed.
(Over) all these encampments of angels these seven overseers
rule, to dispatch (them) for every (sort of) business so that
they will hasten and bring success.

These are the names of the seven overseers who sit upon
(the) seven thrones: the name of the first is 'WRPNY'L, and the
name of the second is TYGRH, and the name of the third is DNHL,
and the name of the fourth is KLMYY', the name of the fifth is
'SYMWR, the name of the sixth is PSKR, the name of the seventh
is BW'L. And all of them were created from fire and their
10   appearance is like fire, and their fire is blazing, for from
fire they emerged.

And without permission, (the angels who serve them)[3] do
not go out to engage in magical actions. (They wait) until a
command comes to them from (one of) the seven overseers, the

---

[1] *Shamayim* is the common Hebrew word for heaven or sky.

[2] Or perhaps "by their letters (of their names)."

[3] Inserted by Ms. ר (Sefer Raziel) and aids the translation.

21

occupants of the thrones, who rule over them. For they are
subject to the will (of the overseers) and go about (only) with
their permission. And each and every one of them goes to his
work determined to act quickly in any affair on which he may be
sent, whether for good or for evil, whether for superfluity or
for shortage, whether for war or for peace. And all of them

15   are to be called by the names (given them) from the day they
were created.

　　　And these are the names of the seven encampments which
serve the seven overseers (for each encampment serves one of
the overseers).

And these are the names of the angels of the first encampment who serve 'WRPNY'L:

BWMDY	DMN'	'NWK	'LPY
'MWK	QṬYBY'	PṬRWPY	GMTY
P''WR	NRNTQ	RQHTY	'WRNH
M'WT	PRWKH	'QYL'H	TRQWYH
BRWQ	SḤRWR'	'TNNY	GYL'N
TKT	'RNWB	'ŚMY	YWṢŚ
KPWN	KRBY	GYRŠWM	PRY'N
ŚŚM^{c}	'BB'	NTN'L	'R'L
'NYP	TRW'WR	^{c}BDY'L	YWWN
'LWN	MW'L	LLP	YḤSPT
RḤGL	RWM'PY	YKTY	'RNY'L
PWBWN	KDY'L	ZKRY'L	'GDLN
MYG'L	G'WPR	KRTH	KYLDH
DYGL	'LNW	TYRLY	SBLH
'BY'L	'L	KSYL	SYQMH
'ŚBH	YWTNH	R'LKH	ḤLY'N
'PTY'L	TY'MY'L	'L'L	NTY'L
'PYKH	TLGY'L	N^{c}NH	'STY'L

These are the angels who are obedient in every matter during the first and second year of the fifteen year cycle of the reckoning of the Greek kings.[4] If you wish to perform an

---

[4]Probably a reference to the Roman indictions. See Margalioth, Sepher 24. If we suppose that this reference to the use of indictions is by the government in Constantinople, then the terminus a quo for the cosmological framework is 312 C.E. The Egyptian dating would give us a terminus a quo of 297 C.E.

act of healing, arise in the first or second hour of the night

30   and take with you[5] myrrh and frankincense. This (is to be)

put[6] on burning coals (while saying) the name of the angel

who rules over the first encampment, who is called 'WRPNY'L,

and say there, seven times, (the names of the) seventy-two[7]

angels who serve before him, and say as follows:

> *I, N the son of N beseech you that you will*
> *give me success in healing N the son of N.*

And anyone for whom you ask, whether in writing or

verbally, will be healed. Purify yourself from all impurity

and cleanse your flesh from all carnality and then you will

succeed.

---

[5]Literally, "in your hand."

[6]Margalioth suggests reading וְהוּא נֹתֵן for וְהוּא נֹתָן.   Possibly
וְהוּא נִיתָן.

[7]Ms. א refers to a list of only seventy names.

35   These are the names of the angels of the second encampment

who serve TYGRH:

'KSTR	MRSWM	BRKYB	KMSW
'STYB	KRYT.'L	'DYR	GB'
'QRB'	'NBWR	KBYR	TYLH
BRYTWR	TRTM	NTPY'L	PRY'L
TRWHWN	SLHBYN	'SLB'	MSTWB
GRHT'	HGR'	'YTMY'L	HGL
LGH	MNYTY'L	TNYMY'L	'YKRYT
'BRYT'	RKYL'L	HSTK	PPTS
40 'STYRWP	'WDY'L	'SBYR	MLKY'L
'RWS	DSWW'	HMK	TRGH
ZMBWT	HSNYPLPT	SWW'	'SPWR
'RQ	QNWMY'L	NHY'L	GDY'L
'DQ	YMWMY'L	PRWG	DHGY'L
DGRY'L	'GRY'L	'RWNWR	DWNRNY'
DLKT	TBL	TLY'L	'LY'L
MWT'R	'LPY'L	PYTPR'	LPWM
'WR	TMR	'DLY'L	'STWRYN
'ZWTY	'YSTWRTY	D'WBYT	BRGMY
DMWMY'L	DYGR'	'BYB'L	PRWTY'L
45 QWMY'L	DGWGR'	DLGY'L	PDWTY'L

These are the angels who are full of anger and wrath[8] and

who have been put in charge of every matter of combat and war

and are prepared to torment and torture a man to death.   There

---

[8]Reading חמה instead of חימה.

is no mercy in them but they (wish) only to take revenge and
to punish him who is delivered into their hands. And if you
wish to send them against your enemy, or against your creditor,
50   or to capsize a ship, or to fell a fortified wall,[9] or against
any business of your enemies, to damage and destroy, whether you
desire to exile him, or to make him bedridden, or to blind him
or to lame him,[10] or to grieve him in any thing (do as follows):
Take[11] water from seven springs on the seventh day of the month,
in the seventh hour of the day, in seven unfired pottery
vessels,[12] and do not mix them[13] with one another. Expose
55   them beneath the stars for seven nights; and on the seventh
night take a glass vial,[14] (and say over it) the name of your
adversary, and pour the water (from the seven unfired pottery
vessels) into it, then break the pottery vessels and throw
(the pieces) to the east, north, west, and south,[15] and say
thus to the four directions:[16]

---

[9]Probably a walled house as found in the later Roman empire.
That it is the wall of a house which is meant is clear
from 1:77.

[10]Literally,"to smite the light of his eyes...to bind
his feet."

[11]Literally,"take in your hand."

[12]Cf. PGM IV:3210f.

[13]I.e., the waters from the different springs.

[14]Cf. PGM IV:222; IV:3210   φιάλη.

[15]Literally,"to the four winds of the heavens."

[16]Literally,"winds."

HHGRYT who dwell in the east, [17] *SRWKYT who
dwell in the north, ᶜWLPH who dwell in the west,
KRDY who dwell in the south, accept from my hand
at this time that which I throw to you, to affect* [18]
60   *N son of N, to break his bones, to crush all his
limbs, and to shatter his conceited power, as
these pottery vessels are broken. And may there
be no recovery for him* [19] *just as there is no repair
for these pottery vessels.*

Then take the vial of water [20] and repeat over it the

names of these angels and the name of the overseer, who is

TYGRH and say thus:

*I deliver to you, angels of anger and wrath, N
son of N, that you will strangle him and destroy him
65   and his appearance,* [21] *make him bedridden, diminish his
wealth, annul the intentions of his heart, blow away
his thought and his knowledge and cause him to waste
away continually until he approaches death.*

If you wish to exile him conclude the formula thus:

*That you will exile him and banish him from his
children and his home and he will have nothing left.*

If he is one to whom you are in debt, conclude (the

formula) thus:

*That you will plug his mouth and make his
planning vain and he will not think of me, nor
speak of me; and when I pass in front of him,
he will not see me.*

70   If (the rite is) for a ship [22] say thus:

---

[17] Literally,"in the east wind," et. al.

[18] Literally,"for the name of."

[19] Margalioth has "for them" and records no variant but the
context requires "for him."

[20] Reading של מים instead of שלמים .

[21] I. e., so that the body will no longer be recognizable.

[22] Either your enemy's ship or one on which he is.

> *I adjure you angels of wrath and destruction,*
> *that you will rise up against the ship of N son of*
> *N and that you not permit it to sail from any place.*
> *But if[23] wind (sufficient) for sailing[24] come to*
> *it, then let (the wind) carry it out to sea and*
> *shake it (so it sinks) in the midst of the sea and*
> *let neither man nor cargo be saved from it.*

If you wish to fell a fortified wall say thus:

75

> *I adjure you, angels of fury, wrath, and anger,*
> *that you will go with the force of your power and*
> *fell the wall of N son of N. Smite it to dust and*
> *let it be overturned like the ruins of Sodom and*
> *Gemorah, and let no man place stone upon stone on*
> *the place[25] (where the wall was); if it be built*
> *during the day, let it be overturned at night.*

Then pour out (the water) upon the four corners of the

house. (In a like manner) if you wish to make your enemy

bedridden, or to destroy his appearance, or to (do) any

grievous thing, pour the water upon his doorstep. If (you

wish) to exile him, pour out the water to the four directions.

80   If (you wish) to bind your creditor, throw the water on his

garments. And if (you wish) to sink a ship, cast the vial

and its water in the midst of the ship (while saying) the

name of the ship and its master. And if you wish to overturn

a wall, dig at the four corners of the wall and divide the

water among (the four corners). (Use the water) thus in each

case. Do it in (a state of) purity and then you will succeed.

---

[23]Reading ואלו for ולא.

[24]Possibly read מנהיג with Ms. ק , a leading wind."

[25]Reading במקומה with Ms. פ for בקומה . Possibly בחומה,
"on the wall."

These are the names of the angels who serve DNHL[26] in

the third encampment:

85	'WGRBBW	'WBS'L	BRTWBY'L	KLWBY'L
	RHBY'L	'WHY'L	KRBTWN	KRB'
	D'YNWT	'YNYK	'BYRM	'TGL'
	'WTWT	'ŚTNW'L	'ŠPR	TGRY'L
	'MYK'L	'TDŚW	'WRY'L	'RMWD
	'STWN	'K'L	'N'WR	'SKYR'
	LBY'L	'LᶜŚH	HSNY'L	LMWŚY
	'DWT	TYRWM	'LPY	'YMYK
	'RGL'	MYG'L	'LY'L	MDNY'L

90   These angels tell everyone who, in purity, gains power

over them, what will happen on the earth in each and every

year, whether for plenty or for famine, whether rains will be

abundant or sparse, and whether there will be a dearth and

whether there will be produce, and whether locusts will come

and whether there will be strife among kings, and whether a

sword will come among the great men of the kingdom,[27] and

whether death or suffering will befall mankind.

        If you wish to know and understand what will be in each

95   and every year, take a hieratic papyrus[28] and cut it into

---

[26] Probably a variant of Daniel or Danel, both of which are found
as divine angelic names.

[27] This seems to imply either strife or execution.

[28] ירטיקון , i.e., ἱερατικόν - a hieretic sheet of papyrus.
"Hieratic" (priestly) here refers especially to the Egyptian
priests who were famed for their magic and from whence came the
types of writing and paper that they used and were thought
suitable for magical operations.

slips) and write in hieratic with a mixture of ink and

myrrh[29] each and every possibility separately.[30] Then

take a new flask and put in it spikenard oil[31] and throw in

the written slips[32] (as well); then stand facing the sun[33]

when he comes forth from his bridal chamber[34] and say:

100
>   *I adjure you O sun that shines on the earth, in*
>   *the name of the angels who make men of knowledge*
>   *understand and comprehend wisdom and secrets, that*
>   *you will do what I ask and make known to me what will*
>   *be in this year--do not conceal a thing from me.*

And you will adjure (the sun with) this adjuration for

three days, three times[35] and the third time you will scruti-

nize the oil. Notice everything brought up upon the face of

the oil, that is what will happen in that year. If two

---

[29] בזמירנה מלנון for σμορνό-μέλαν(ον) - a special ink used
for magical purposes.

[30] I.e., one possibility on each slip.

[31] Cf. PGM I:278.

[32] Literally, "things."

[33] Cf. PGM II:87; III:325; IV:260; V:237.

[34] Here the text has צאתה מחופתה . If the final ה 's
were taken as feminine terminations (which they usually are)
this would mean "when she comes forth from her bridal chamber."
However, the sun is most often masculine. The verb forms and
pronouns referring to the sun in this context are all masculine.
Therefore, it is more plausible to explain these endings as
Aramaizing spellings for the masculine termination ו .

[35] Literally, "3 days 3 times." Possibly once a day or three
times each day.

possibilities come up, then there will be (these) two and

if three come up, there will be three. Afterwards, take

105   the oil and burn it while saying the names of the angels

that serve in this encampment. And (as for) the rest of

all the written (slips), hide them[36] in a wall or in a

window. And so, (as in) every operation, act in purity,

and you will succeed.

---

[36] Reading גניזם for יגביזם, implying a ritual burial or
storage both here and elsewhere in the text.

These are the names of the angels who serve KLMYYH[37] in the fourth encampment:

'BRYH	'YMRHY	DMN'Y	'MNHR
Y'MNWK	PṬKY'	ṬWBY'L	GWLY'L
'WPRY	GMTY	'WRNY'L	PRYKYHW
Y'RN	LṬMY'L	'WRYṬ	TYMWGW
'NMRY	'LMYNY'L	YKMṬW	SṬRṬW
ṢB^{c}QNY	BWRTY'S	RSPWT	KRSWN
'M'P	WP'ṬN'	'Ḥ'L	S'BY'L
BLQYR	PKHWR	HSTR	STRY'L
'LYSS	ḤLSY'L	ṬRSPW	QRSṬWS
MLKY'L	'RDQ	ḤSDY'L	'ḤSP
'MY'L	PRNWS	GDY'L	SBYB'L

These are the angels[38] who bring around[39] the opinion of the king and the good will of the nobles, chiefs, and leaders of the kingdom, directing and bestowing favor and mercy upon all who arise in purity to request anything from them. Perform this rite zealously and you will succeed.

If you wish to turn the king's opinion to your favor, or (that of) the chief of the army, or a rich man, or a ruler, or a judge of a city, or all the citizens of the state, or

---

[37] Here spelled with a ה instead of a א as in 1:8. The manuscripts show other variations, BLMY', GDYMYY'.

[38] Perhaps the 36th angel comes from Χριστός. Cf. 1:130.

[39] משובבים is possibly from שבב . Margalioth suggests amending to משרתים or שתסובב. Possibly amend to מסבבים. Cf. 1:127 שתסובו.

(if you wish to change) the heart of a great or wealthy

woman, or the heart of a beautiful[40] woman, (do this). Take

a lion cub and slaughter it with a bronze knife and catch its

120   blood and tear out its heart[41] and put its blood in the midst

(of the heart) and write the names of these (above mentioned)

angels in blood upon the skin between its eyes; then wash it

out with wine three years old and mix (the wine) with the

blood.

Then take three of the chief spices, istorgon[42] and

myrrh and musk,[43] and stand clean and pure, facing the

brilliant star[44] and put the spices on the fire; then take

in your hand the cup in which are the wine and the blood and

say (this spell over it while burning the incense) and call

125   on the name of the overseer and the names of the angels of

this encampment. (Do this) twenty-one times over the blood

and over the wine and say to the brilliant star, the name

(of the star) which is that of Aphrodite, three hundred

(times)[45] and (the name of the) angel ḤSDY'L (and then say):

---

[40]Reading יופיה for ביופיה.

[41]Cf. PGM III:425 and DMP 25:27, p. 155.

[42]איסטרקון is probably στύραξ (styrax), a fragrant gum.

[43]ושורה דמושך. If Margalioth is correct in assuming that מושך
is a transliteration of the Persian musk and the Greek moschos,
then the ד implies an Aramaic form making שורה the Aramaic
"chain" or "chord." Margalioth points out the similarity
between the Arabic targum of SHR which reads WSWRT 'LMSK and
the Arabic targum of the Song of Songs 1:13 which reads SRH
'LMSK. Thus the targum renders "bag of myrrh" as "bag of musk."

[44]I.e., Aphrodite-Venus. Cf. 1:126.

[45]שאפרודיטי Cf. PGM IV:2891. Margalioth suggests deletion of
the ש.

*I adjure you in the name of the angels of
the fourth encampment who serve KLMY' that you
bring around for me King N so that the heart of
his army and the heart of his ministers (will be)
in my hand, I, N son of N, and I will find favor
and mercy before him and he will do what I want
and ask, whenever I ask (anything) from him.*

130   When you finish repeating the adjuration twenty-one times,

look up and you will see (something) like a coal of fire

descending into the blood and wine.[46]

If you wish to enter the presence of the king or any (great)

man, or a judge, wash yourself with "living" water[47] and take

some of the blood and some of the wine and anoint your body,

and place the lion's heart over your heart. If (you wish) to

135   bring around the citizens of the city[48] take the lion's heart

and hide it in the midst of the city, and write on a (piece of)

gold foil[49] the (name of) the overseer and (the names of the

angels of) his encampment and say thus:

*You angels who go around and circulate in the
world, bring around (to me) all the citizens of this
city, great and small, old and young, lowly and
distinguished. Let the fear and terror of me be over
them as the terror of the lion is over all the animals.
And as this heart is mute while I am speaking, so let*
140   *all of them listen to me, and let none of the children
of Adam and Eve be able to speak against me.*

---

[46]Cf. the notion of the descent of the holy spirit, body and
blood of Christ into the bread and wine of the Eucharist. Note
the use of QRSTWS in the angelic list of this encampment. Cf.
4 Ezra 14:39.

[47]מים חיים, "living water," i.e., water from a stream or spring,
not from a cistern.

[48]מדינה is here translated as "city" as it fits the sense better
than "state" which was used in 1:118.

[49]ציץ, gold plate, metal disc, or *lamella*, often used for making
amulets.

Hide the heart in the middle of the city and go into seclusion[50] for three days and after three days appear in the city. (For this occasion) put some of the lion's blood under the soles of your feet.

If you wish to bind yourself to the heart of a great or wealthy woman[51] take some perspiration from your face (and put it) in a new glass vessel; then write on it, (i.e.) on a

145 tin *lamella*,[52] the name of the overseer and the names of the angels, and throw (the tin *lamella*) in the midst (of the flask) and say thus over the perspiration of your face:

> *I adjure you angels of favor and knowledge, that you will turn (to me) the heart of N daughter of N and let her do nothing without me, and let her heart be (joined) with my heart in love.*

Take the new flask and bury it under her doorstep[53]

and say:

> *Just as a woman will return to the infant of her womb, so this N will return to me to love me from this*
150 > *day and forever.*

This should be written[54] at the full moon.

---

[50]Literally "hide your face."

[51]This love potion is independent of the previous use of the lion's blood.

[52]Either the phrase "on it" or "on a tin *lamella*" seems to be a repetitive addition.

[53]Literally "the place of her coming in and going out."

[54]Reading יכתב for יכתוב .

These are the angels who serve 'SYMWR in the fifth

encampment:

BTW'R	ŠKYNTTK	'DWM'	TQW
MQP'	LHB'	^{c}LY	^{c}ZY
ŠKNY'L	KNWR	BNŚ	QRB'
SRK	HLŚY'L	HRMN^c	^{c}BR
HWD	MLKYH	PR^{c}TWP	'D^{c}T
QWP	MNMLK	DYNMWR	'LPNṬWS
DYDRYWK	KLNH	NYNḤY'	DSNḤY'
MLGDM	DYMHN	LYBRNK	TTQHH
'PNY'L	ZBYṬWR	DKNSWR	RMGDL
LHTQWP	^{c}LY	GDGDL	PRWṢ
MSRWṢ	KDYR	MWS	DYQN'
NŚR	TWB	DRWMY'L	DYR'Z
DMWL'	DYDY'L	Ṭ^{c}Y	KRM
'TR	^{c}QB	HWNMWR'	'NQYW
GZRY'L	ṢBY'L	ṢBYWD^c	YYQR
'DWT	RGBY'L		

155 (line marker by MLGDM)

These are the angels who obey (you) during the night (if

160 you wish) to speak with the moon or the stars or to question a

ghost or to speak with the spirits.

If you wish to speak with the moon or with the stars about

any matter, take a white cock and fine flour, then slaughter

the cock[55] (so that its blood is caught) in "living water."[56]

Knead the flour with the water and blood and make three cakes

_____

[55]Reading שכוֹ for טכוֹ.

[56]Cf. above, note 47.

and place them in the sun, and write on them with the blood

the name(s) of (the angels of) the fifth encampment and the

name of its overseer and put the three of them on a table of

165   myrtle wood, stand[57] facing the moon or facing the stars

and say:

> *I adjure you to bring the planet of N and his star*
> *near to the star and planet of N, so his love will be*
> *tied with the heart of N son of N.*[58]

Or say:

> *Place fire from your fire in the heart of this N*
> *(masc.) or that N (fem.) so she will abandon her*
> *father's and mother's house[59] because of love for*
> *this N (masc.) son of N (fem.).*[60]

Then take two of the cakes and place them with the cock

in a new flask; then seal its mouth with wax and hide the

flask in a place not exposed to the sun.[61]

170   If you wish acts of kindness (to be done to you); take the

---

[57]Reading עוֹמֵד for אִימֵר.

[58]The grammar here is most confusing. It would seem that the
first clause (1:165,166) is a homosexual love formula and that
the second (1:166,167) is bi-sexual. Another possibility is
that the first clause uses a common masculine to imply that
the formula could be used by any party. The fact that the
second clause specifically provides for attraction of either a
male or a female to a man seems, however, to imply that the
first clause is indeed homosexual. The question is influenced
by our rendering of וְאָמוּר . Does it imply a new formula or a
continuation of the former? Cf. its usage in the first
firmament, second encampment (p.27). Also compare DMP 22:40
p.143; and PGM IV:345f. and 1480f.

[59]Literally "her father's house and her mother." This is
probably a colloquial construction.

[60]Note the definition of an individual by specification of
his mother. This is common in Egyptian magic texts and used
often in SHR. A common saying was, "the mother is certainly
known, the father uncertain."

[61]See also 2:173. Cf. PGM VII:915. καὶ ἡλίῳ μὴ δείξῃς

remaining cake, crumble it, and place it in aged wine in a

glass cup, and say the name(s) of the angels in the presence

of the moon and the stars and continue thus:

> *I adjure you that you will give favor, kindness,*
> *and affection, to N, from the favor, kindness, and*
> *affection that radiate from your countenance. (Give*
> *them to) me, N son of N, so that I will find favor,*
> *kindness, affection, and honor in the eyes of every man.*

Then blow into the wind and wash your face each dawn,

175   for nine days, with the wine and the cake crumbled in it.

If you wish to question a ghost; stand facing a tomb and

repeat the names of the angels of the fifth encampment (while

holding) in your hand a new flask (containing) oil and honey

mixed together and say thus:

> *I adjure you O spirit of the ram bearer[62] who*
> *dwell among the graves upon the bones of the dead, that*
> *you will accept from my hand this offering and do my*
180 > *will and bring me (the spirit of) N son of N who is*
> *dead. Raise him up so that he will speak to me without*
> *fear and tell me true things without concealment.[63]*
> *Let me not be afraid of him and let him tell me (for)*
> *my question, (the answer) I need from him.*

He should appear immediately. But if he does not, repeat

the adjuration a second time (and) up to three times. When he

appears set the flask before him and after this speak your

words while holding a twig of myrtle in your hand.[64]   If you

185   wish to release him, strike him three times with the myrtle and

pour out the oil and honey, and break the cup, and throw the

myrtle from your hand, and return home by a different route.

------

[62] קריפורייא , i.e., Κρισφόρος or Hermes.

[63] Cf. PGM IV:1034. Spirits do not always tell the truth.

[64] The flask and myrtle are to protect the person reciting the
incantation. Cf. Goodenough, Symbols 2.174.

If you wish to speak with the spirits, go out to "the place of the killed"[65] and call out there in a singsong, whimpering way:

> *I adjure you in the name of the angels who serve in the fifth encampment, and in the name of the overseer who is over them, who is 'SYMWR, that you will hear me at this time and send me the spirit of ḤGRGYRWT.[66] She shall go according to my will for whatever I send her and shall obey me in everything until such and such a time.*

190

If you see opposite you a column of smoke, speak your words and send (her) for whatever purpose you wish.

These are the names of the angels who serve PSKR in the sixth encampment:

'ZY'L	'RBY'L	TRYPWN	PWKBWS
PSTMR	LYNNY'L	QRWNYDN	ŠWKDWN
SLBYDM	ᶜMY'L	ᶜWZY'L	PNY'L
TRMY'L	HMMY'L	SRMY'L	NYMMWS
NWDNYY'	B'RYB'	ZWNNWM	ḤSTW'L
SDRY'L	HWPNY'WN	QDMY'L	KPNYY'
'RMY'L	ᶜDMWN	HRMWR	ṢPLY'L
SPRY'L	QHNY'L	ŠBKYRY'	'RMWNYS
TWPWMWS	PSSY'L	HTPY'L	PRSWMWN
NHLY'L			

195

These are the angels of might who gird on power and strength to run from place to place and to fly in all corners

200

---

[65] Possibly the place of public executions or the place where executed criminals were buried, or a place where multiple murders had been committed.

[66] חגרגירות . The reference is unknown. Possibly from "Hagar the Proselyte," הגר גירות.

of the earth to return a man, a fugitive, either a slave who

fled or a thief who fled. (If you wish to catch a fugitive)

take four copper *lamellae* and write upon each and every one of

them the name of the man and the name of his mother,[67] the name

of the overseer, PSKR, and the names of the angels who serve

him, and say:

205

> *I charge you, angels of might, to seize N son of*
> *N, wherever he goes and wherever he dwells, whether in*
> *a city or in a country, whether at sea or on land,*
> *whether eating or drinking. You shall make him fly like*
> *a flying bird and bring him against his will, and not*
> *let him linger one moment, whether by day or by night.*

Then take (the) four copper *lamellae* and hide them in

the four directions[68] whether in the city or in the country.

These are the names of the angels who serve BW'L in the

seventh encampment:

210 NWHRY'L	DBB'L	DYMTMR	DB'L
MḤṢYN	''WR	DY'M	BBYT'L
SRWR'	'HGYYH	PRWPY'L	MKSY'L
ᶜLZY'L	TKWRKS	QRWMY'L	RMY'L
LḤSWN	SLḤY'L	'HY'L	'KR
'WBR	SRWGY'L	YDW'L	ṠMṠY'L
ṠPṬY'L	RHBY'	'HMWD'	MRMRYN
'NWK	'LPRṬ	'WMYGR'	QRWKNS
SRPY'L	GDRY'L	'RDWD'	PWRTNY'L
'GMY'L	RHTY'L	DYTRWN	ḤZ'L
215 PTW'L	GLGL'	DMNSR	ZZY'L

---

[67]On descent through the mother, cf. First Firmament, note 60
(p. 37).

[68]I.e., towards the north, south, east, and west.

These are the names of the angels in charge of dreaming, to make anyone who approaches them in purity know what the dream (was) and what its interpretation is.

If the king, or the head of the city, or governor, or your friend summons you and you want to give him an answer from your wisdom, say to him, "I will make known to you what is in your heart concerning me." (or "what you thought about me," or

220 "what you want to do," or "what is the interpretation of your dream.")[69] "Give me a period of three days and I will make known to you all that is in your heart." Then go out on Sunday to the sea shore or to a river bank during the third hour of the night. Wear a new cloak[70] and do not eat (the meat of) any animal,[71] nor anything which yields blood (when slaughtered), and do not drink wine. Take myrrh and pure frankincense and place them on burning coals in a new earthen vessel, and turn your face toward the water and repeat three

225 times the name of the overseer with the name(s) of the angels of the encampment. When you see a pillar of fire between heaven and earth say thus:

---

[69] The magician is to choose the appropriate phrase. Cf. PGM I:175.

[70] אסטולי i.e., στολή. Semetic pronounciation often avoids double consonants by the introduction of vowels.

[71] Hebrew דקה . Margalioth reads דגה , fish, which might be possible in sympathy with "the river." But see 2:8 and notes. Furthermore the next phrase, "anything which issues blood" would not classically apply to "fish." In 5:35 we read "both small animals and all that yields blood *even* fish." Thus it seems that SHR would go out of its way to make the distinction if it was appropriate.

*I adjure you by the One who measured the waters
in the palm of His hand and rebuked the waters so that
they fled from Him, and made winds flying in the air
his personal servants, as a fiery flame, who rebuked
the sea and dried it up, and made rivers a desert,[72]
by His name and by its letters, I adjure you, and by
the names of the angels[73] of the seventh encampment
who serve BW'L, that you make known to me what is in
the heart of N son of N and what is his desire, and
what is the interpretation of his dream and what is
his thought.*

230

Do likewise on the second and third nights and you will see
that a pillar of fire will appear to you with a cloud on it like
the image of a man.[74] Question him and he will tell you whatever you ask. And if you wish to release him throw some of the
water, from the sea or the river by which you are standing,
toward heaven three times and say under your breath:[75]

235

*Invisible Lord BW'L, sufficient to our need, the
perfect shield bearer,[76] I free you, I free you, subside
and return to your (heavenly) course.*

Say this seven times. Perform the entire rite in purity
and you will succeed.

These are the names of the seven spirits who serve in the
firmament called *Shamayim.*

PEACE.

---

[72]The adjuration is a combination of Isa 40:12; Ps 104:4;
107:33; and Nah 1:4.

[73]Reading שמות for ז בשם ,i.e.,"the names of" for "the name
of seven" angels, since there are 44 angels in this encampment.

[74]Cf. Ezek 1:4.

[75]Cf. PGM III:108.

[76]With Margalioth, Sepher 80, following the transcription of
Morton Smith. אורודי גרי/באל פוט/מוס סרגרי טליגוס אספדיפורוס
ἀόρατε κύριε Βουῆλ, ποτ' ἡμᾶς ἄρκιε, τελικὸς
ἀσπιδηφόρος.

The second firmament is called "heaven of heavens."[1] In
it are frost and fog[2] and treasuries of snow and treasuries
of hail, angels of fire and angels of moisture[3] and spirits
of terror and spirits of dread. The firmament is full of fear,
for within it are innumerable angels constituting armies upon
armies and over them are officers and overseers. Within the
firmament are twelve steps[4] and on each and every step stand
angels in their splendor, and over them is one high official
over another. Nevertheless, for human affairs, they are
obedient to everyone who approaches them in purity.

If you wish to ask something of any who stand on the steps
of the second firmament, cleanse yourself for three weeks from
all fruit of the palm,[5] from all kinds of animals, small and
large,[6] from wine, from (all) types of fish and from all
(animals) that yield blood (when slaughtered); and do not
approach a woman in her impurity,[7] and do not touch anything

---

[1] שמי שמים, a common designation in mystical literature for the
second heaven.

[2] קטור וקטור. קטור ּ - "smoke." Here it seems to imply mist or
fog in parallel to frost, snow, hail, etc.

[3] Reading זיעה, i.e., "moisture" with Mss. ה and א instead of
זיע, i.e., "trembling."

[4] מעלות, i.e., steps, levels, divisions.

[5] Reading דקל for דקה with Margalioth.

[6] דקה וגסה, i.e., small and large animals. This is a common
distinction found in Rabbinic literature between sheep and
goats as opposed to cattle.

[7] Cf. Ezek 18:6.

which has died,[8] and do not come near a leper or one afflicted
10   by venereal discharge, even accidental, and guard your mouth

from every evil word and from every sin; and sanctify yourself

from every sin.

Upon the first step stand these:

'ḤMRY'L	HDRY'L	RṢY'L	HSᶜY'L
DMYMY'L	ZBDY'L	RNZY'L	ᶜNṠ'L
KTBR'L			

These, their station is on the first step. They stand in

terror, cloaked in wrath, girded with dread, surrounded by
15   trembling, their raiment like an image of fire, their faces

like the appearance of lightning, and their mouths never cease

(to utter) mighty words. Nevertheless, their voice is not

heard, for their task is to silence, to frighten, and to

terrify anyone who opposes the man who calls on them in purity.

If you wish to silence a great and powerful people, or a

governor, or a judge, or the citizens of a city, or of a state,

take a handful of ashes from beneath the bread offering[9] of an
20   idol and say over it backwards[10] seven times the names of the

angels written above (as standing) on the first step, and say:

> I ask from you, angels of silence, that in this
> place, you silence every mouth and every heart of the
> children of Adam and Eve who arise against me to (say)
> anything evil. Let their mouths utter good things about

---

[8]Cf. Lev 21:11.

[9]Cf. Testament of Job 7. Here reading פם for פאה

[10]מפרע, possibly "out of order" or "irregularly," but most
likely "backwards" the normal meaning. Saying things backwards
is a well-known magical practice.

me and let me be exonerated in my lawsuit; do not
permit any mouth to speak evil about me.[11]

Then sprinkle the ashes, either in the city or in the

25   state, either before the governor or before the judge, and

you will be exonerated.

Upon the second step stand these:

ᶜZZY'L	HNN'L	PSSY'L	YŠᶜY'L
DLQY'L	'RPD'	MR'WT	RYPYPYS
'MNY'L	NHMY'L	PRZYRWM	ᶜNB'L

These, their station is on the second step. They stand with

strength, filled with might, surrounded with love, and in

their presence fire burns, and they hasten to bring the

30   (ruling) planets of the sons of man into conjunction for love.

If you wish to put the love of a man into the heart of a

woman, or to arrange for a poor man to wed a rich woman, take

two copper *lamellae* and write upon them, on both sides, the

names of these angels, and the name of the man and the name of

the woman and say thus:

> *I ask of you, angels who rule the fates of the*
> *children of Adam and Eve, that you do my will and*
> *bring in conjunction the planet of N son of N into*
> *conjunction with (the planet of) the woman N daughter*
> *of N. Let him find favor and affection in her eyes*

35   > *and do not let her belong to any man except him.*

Place one (*lamella*) in a fiery furnace and the other in

her ritual bath.[12] Do this on the twenty-ninth of the month

---

[11]In this formula note that two angelic names, הסעיאל and
דמימיאל which are derived from verbs meaning "to silence"
(הס,דממ).

[12]By Rabbinic law, if the woman uses a ritual bath, *mikvah*,
she is either about to be married or married, thus limiting
the formula's usefulness to bridegrooms, husbands and

when the moon has waned completely. Take care to keep

yourself from intercourse, from wine, and from all (kinds of)

meat for three days.[13]

Upon the third step stand these:

YHW'L	D^{C}YHW	'LY'L	BRKY'L
^{C}LY	SPWM	PNYMWR	'L^{C}ZR
GBLY'L	KMŚY'L	'WDH'L	Y^{C}Ṣ'L
RPPY'L	PSPY'L		

40

14

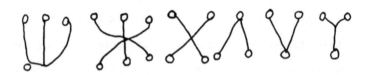

---

adulterers. Since we do not know in what circles this document
circulated, it is of course impossible to draw a definite conclusion about its intended use.

[13]Since the introduction to the Second Firmament gives general
rules of abstinence to follow before using the formulas of the
Second Firmament, we must assume that these rules are to be
followed after the spell has been cast in order to insure
effectiveness.

[14]These characters appear here in Ms. ח . Such symbols,
which were used to enhance the power of amulets and spells,
were common both in the Greek and Jewish worlds. Cf. Margalioth,
Sepher 4; PGM IV:2706; VII:810, 816, 860, 922. These
characters are also reproduced in the sixth step of the Second
Firmament and in the Third Firmament. Full magical alphabets
coalesce at a later date. Cf. Robert Ambelain, La Kabbale
Pratique (Paris: Edition Niclaus, 1951), or the chart
reproduced in Gustav Davidson, A Dictionary of Angels (London:
Macmillan, 1967) 335. The use of ringed symbols may derive
from the punch writing on Greek allotment plates which were
worn in a similar fashion to amulets. Cf. John H. Kroll,
Athenian Bronze Allotment Plates (Cambridge, Mass: Harvard
University Press, 1972).

These, their station is on the third step, for their
function is to shake and agitate the hearts of men and to make
void their intentions and nullify their thoughts. Dread is
theirs and fear where they walk, and their appearance is (full)
of wrath, and they are exceedingly harsh and mighty men of war,
and fear goes before them and trembling after them,[15] and
they roar and cause trembling as they go shaking[16] (the world),
and their voice is like the voice of thunder and in their hands
are rods of fire and their faces are like sparks of fire and
45   fire comes forth from their eyes, and all of them are ready
to nullify and make void (whatever they are asked to).

If you wish to nullify a great man's intentions towards
you, or the thoughts of an army officer, or the intentions of
military men, or any other evil intentions or thoughts
(directed against you); go out at midnight when the moon is
full, barefoot,[17] and pure, and wrapped in a new cloak.[18]
Stand under the moon and say twenty-one times the names of the
angels written above, (those) who stand on the third step of
50   the "heaven of heavens," and say:

> *Moon, Moon, O Moon, bring my words before the angels*
> *who stand upon the third step: nullify the thought*
> *concerning me of N son of N and the intention of his*
> *heart and his plot. Let his mouth be unable to speak*

---

[15]This calls to mind the figure of Ares and his attendants.

[16]רעש , commonly associated with earthquakes.

[17]The text reads יחיד, i.e., "alone." Margalioth reads יחף
"barefoot." This is justified by other magical texts of a
similar nature.

[18]אסטולי , i.e., στολή. Cf. First Firmament, note 70 (p.41).

against me, destroy his knowledge, and thwart his
intentions, and let his purpose[19] be devastated,
so that every time he sees me he will be filled
with love for me, and let him be changed so that he
becomes my friend, and let him not remember any
hatred of me, and let me find favor and affection
in his eyes.

55   Then write (the names of) the angels and these (following)

characters[20] upon a silver *lamella*; put them on a tablet over

your heart,[21] and during all the days you wear it[22] you shall

succeed.

     Upon the fourth step stand these:

SGRY'L	MLKY'L	'WNBYB	PGRY'L
CNNY'L	KLNMYY'	'WMY'L	MPNWR
KWZZYB'	'LPY'L	PRYBY'L	SCQMYH
KDWMY'L	'SMDC	HWDYH	YHZY'L

These, their station is on the fourth step.[23] They are girded

60   with storm and the sound of their steps is like the sound of

bronze. They fly from the east and turn from the west towards

the gate.[24] They are swift as lightning and fire is around

---

[19]Literally "heart."

[20]והכרקטורים for χαρακτῆρες. Cf. note 14 (p.46).

[21]Reading על לוח על לבבך . This is a recipe for an amulet. The
idea is that you put the silver foil on a stronger tablet and
wear it suspended over your heart (chest).

[22]Literally, "it is upon you."

[23]Note the ninth angel, KWZZYB', and the thirteenth, 'SMDC .
KWZZYB' is most probably Bar Kochba. This would clearly date
the angelology as post 135 CE. 'SMDCis most probably Asmodeus.
Cf. Tob 3:7,17.

[24]פילון for πυλών.

them. They withhold[25] sleep from men, and they can do good

or do evil.

If you wish to give your enemy trouble in sleeping,[26]

take the head of a black dog that never saw light during its

days and take a *lamella* from a strip of (lead) pipe from an

aqueduct,[27] and write upon it (the names of) these angels

and say thus:

> *I hand over to you, angels of disquiet who stand*
65 > *upon the fourth step, the life and the soul and the*
> *spirit of N son of N so that you may tie him in chains*
> *of iron and bind him to a bronze yoke. Do not give*
> *sleep, nor slumber, nor drowsiness to his eyelids;*
> *let him weep and cry like a woman at childbirth, and*
> *do not permit any (other) man to release him (from*
> *this spell).*

Write thus (as above) and put (the inscribed lead

lamella) in the mouth of the dog's head[28] and put wax on its

mouth, and seal (it) with a ring which has a lion (engraved)

70 upon it. Then go and conceal it behind his house or in a

place he frequents.[29]

If you wish to release him (take the dog's head) away

from where it is concealed and remove its seal and withdraw

the text and throw it into a fire, and he will fall asleep

at once. Do this with humility and you will succeed.

---

[25] Literally "separate."

[26] Cf. PGM IV:2943.

[27] פסוכרנופורון for ψυχροφόρον . Cf. PGM VII:397.

[28] Cf. PGM XXXVI:232,370.

[29] Literally "a place in which he goes and comes." His door-step is most likely, as this was a popular and effective place for magic deposits. Cf. First Firmament, note 53 (p.35).

Upon the fifth step stand these:

QWN'QRY'L	PTWNY'L	NQRY'L	'Y'L
Y'BWTY'W	BBSB'W	BKPY	MBWM
SKTB'Q	'MRY'L	Y'L'L	MKS'BW

75

These are they who stand on the fifth step. They grasp shield
and spear, and brass helmets are on their heads, and their
garments are coats of mail. To their right and left are
(storms) as of hailstones. Trembling (accompanies) their
running and they stride upon rivers of fire, grasping torches,
and hurrying to return an answer, and their mouths never silent
from roaring, and their breath[30] is like flaming fire, and
their fire is blazing (so that) the breath of their mouths

80   kindles fire, for all their actions concern the treasuries of
fire, for from fire they emerged and they are stationed in fire.

If you wish to light an oven in the cold, take a lump of
sulphur (that weighs) about seven shekels[31] and divide it into
the number of compartments in the oven. Then upon each and
every (lump of sulphur) write with a bronze stylus[32] the names
of the angels who stand upon the fifth step and say:

> *I adjure you, angels of fire and angels of flame,*
> *by the King who is a consuming fire, that you shall*
> *stand with me and kindle the oven which is in such*
> *a place, and it shall be that anyone who approaches*
> *it will be amazed at its heat.*

85

---

[30]Perhaps "their spirit," but "breath" is more likely here.

[31]Or possibly 27 shekels exactly. Reading כ''ז.

[32]Reading בעת של נחושת with Mss. ס and ח instead of בעשש נחושת.

Do this in the proven manner[33] and you will succeed.

Then take the sulphur and cast it into each and every burner

of it (the oven) and it (the sulphur) will blaze up strongly.

Every day that you wish to light (the oven) write (as directed)

and cast (the sulphur) into the midst (of the oven).

Upon the sixth step stand these:

'BYHWD	QYTR	ZLQY'L	STRY'L
'DRK	GHLY'L	TMKY'L	SMKYH
RB^{C}Y'L	YWQMY'L	SMYHWD	MHRY'L
DWMY'L	KRKWS	QNZ	QNY'L
KNTWN			

These are they who stand on the sixth step. They behave with

humility, but their faces are full of glory. Their garments

are garments white as light. They stand like giants, awesome

as the scholars of a court,[34] seated in thrones of glory,

trusted to give true (judgments), and in charge of healing.

If you wish to heal a man who has had a stroke and half of

him is dried up, either by an (evil) spirit or by witchcraft,

take spikenard oil and three measures of honey and stand facing

the sun as it rises, repeating three times each day for seven

days the name of the man and the name of his mother and the

names of the angels who stand upon the sixth step. And on the

seventh day take him and stand him naked before the sun, and

smear oil all over his flesh, while burning myrrh, frankincense,

and chosen spices in the sunlight. Then again write upon a

---

[33]דוקמא for δοκιμή, or possibly δόλμα.

[34]Literally, "of a yeshivah" or academy.

silver *lamella* (the names of) these angels of glory with

these characters:[35]

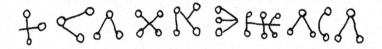

(Write these on the *lamella*) as an amulet and put it on his

neck with a (cord of) asbestos[36] and incense of spices. Write

it thus on the twentieth of the month and you will succeed.

Upon the seventh step stand these:

PTHYH	RZY'L	'GRY'L	HGDY'B
'DRWN	KRQT'	QTYPWR	'BRY'L
ŠTQY'L	^cMY'L	SYKBRDWM	

105 These are they who stand on the seventh step, girt with

strength, their might like a lion. Half of them are like

fire and half of them cold as water. They stand in their

place (and are weakened from their fear).[37] They are wondrous

because of their deeds and no one can comprehend their image,

---

[35]See note 14 above (p.46). The characters given in the text
are from Ms. ה . Ms. ס reads:

[36]אמיניטון for ἀμίαντος i.e. "asbestos." Properly an
adjective meaning "undefiled." Asbestos was used to fashion
magical chains. Cf. PGM XIII:300; and the Fifth Firmament,
line 40 and note 11 (p.76).

[37]The text appears to be corrupt. Compare with lines 157-160
below.

for they come great in stature with sparks of light upon their
eyelids. Those who stand below are unable to look at their
appearance and those, too, who stand above are frightened by
110   their appearance; for they turn to every side and above, and
they move in all four directions.[38]

If you wish to expel from the city every dangerous wild
animal, whether lion, or wolf, or bear, or leopard, or (if you
wish to quell) a river or sea which is rising and washing
against buildings, (do the following). (For the wild animals)
make a bronze image in the likeness of the one (which you
desire to expel) and then make an iron *lamella* and write upon
it, on the obverse and reverse, the names of the angels (of the
seventh step) and bind it upon (the image) and bury it at the
115   entrance of the city and let its face be facing north. If it
is a river or a sea you wish to bind so that it will not come
and flood (the city), make a stone image (of a man), write
(the names of) these angels on two copper *lamellae* and place
them beneath his heels, and make a marble staff and place it
on his shoulder, his right hand grasping the staff and his
left hand open and his face towards the water.[39]

---

[38]This implies that the angels can look in all directions at
once.

[39]This image seems to be forbidden by Rabbinic texts. Cf.
Mishnah Avodah Zarah 3:1; Maimonides, Mishnah Torah on
A.Z. 7:6. Note that there are no spells, rituals, or
sacrifices mentioned to be used when employing this figure.
Perhaps a later hand has deleted them.

Upon the eighth step stand these:

'BRH	BRQY'L	'DWNY'L	^CZRY'L
BRKY'L	^CMY'L	QDŠY'L	MRGY'L
PRW'L	PNY'L	MRBNY'L	MRNYS'L
ŚMY'L	^CMNY'L	MṬN'L	HWD HWD

120

These are they who stand upon the eighth step.[40]
Their appearance is as shining amber, they speak by their
deeds, trembling and fire are in their dwelling place, (their
presence) is filled with fear.[41] They rule the spirits that
wander in the earth, and in a place where their name is invoked
an evil spirit cannot appear.

If you wish to drive off an evil spirit so it will not come
to a woman when she is in childbirth and so it will not kill

125   her child, before the woman's pregnancy write (the names of)
these angels on a golden *lamella* and place it in a silver
tubular case and let her wear it, and at the time of childbirth
take four silver *lamellae* and write upon them (the names of)
the angels and place them in the four sides of the house[42] and
no (evil) spirit will come in.[43]

---

[40]The sixteenth, הוד הוד, is not an angelic name. It is rather
a description of their magnificence. Possibly amend to read
הוד והוד both here and in 2:121.

[41]The text says, "they are filled with fear," but the meaning
is clearly that they frighten those they encounter.

[42]Probably the center of the four walls and not the corners.

[43]Literally "come up," but the meaning is come up into (the
house)."

Upon the ninth step stand these:

GDWDY'L	SKSY'L	TRSWNY'L	NSHY'L
'SDD'	RBNY'	HLYL'L	TWQPY'L
SMKY'L	PDH'L	QRB'	SY'L
PR'L	PTHY'L		

130 is printed to the left of the third row (SMKY'L PDH'L QRB' SY'L).

These are they who stand on the ninth step. Quick and
mighty, flying through the air, their strength is a breastplate
and they appear to have swords in their hands; prepared for
war, grasping bows and holding javelins, they leap forth from
the fire. And they have horses of fire, and the harness of
their chariots is of fire, and terror goes with them wherever
they turn.

If you wish that a man going forth to war be protected from
135 arrow, sword, or any blow, take seven leaves of a bay tree[44]
and write these names on them, two on each and every one of
them, and put them in spikenard oil, and on the day he goes
forth to war, let him smear (the oil) upon his flesh and upon
his sword and his bow and arrows. Again write (the names of
the angels) on a silver *lamella*, put them in a bronze tubular
case, and let him tie it over his heart, then no blow will
touch him.

---

[44]Reading עְרָא for עְר. Cf. Jastrow, Dictionary 1109;
PGM XXIV:15; I:264.

Upon the tenth step stand these:

140	DKRY'L	HRY'L	ṠBQY'L	'TKY'L
	SMYK'L	MRMW'L	QN'L	SPTP
	YH'L	'LSDQ	'KPP	ᶜZM'L
	MKMYK'L	TRKY'L	TBGY'L	

These are they who stand on the tenth step.[45] They have been commanded (to reward) truth. Before them are myriads upon myriads (of angels) holding reed (pens) for fire and writing scrolls uninterruptedly, and recording acquittal for all those who call upon their names, (so that they) will be rescued and saved from forced tribute, the law of the land, and from every death penalty.

145   If you wish to rescue your friend from a bad judgment, or from any difficulty, purify yourself from all impurity, and do not cohabit with a woman for three days; then stand before the sun at the dawn and repeat these names (of these angels) and say:

> *I beseech thee O great angel who art called "sun,"
> who ascend the steps of the firmament, who watch the
> children of men, that you will perform my request and will
> bring my words before the King of Kings of Kings, the*
> 150   *(Holy One) Blessed be He, to whom I pray concerning the
> case of N son of N, who is in trouble and has a bad
> case; and that you will bring over for him, from (God's)
> presence, something good and a time of relief. Let
> those who sought to do him evil be ashamed and let him
> be rescued without injury.*

In addition, write (the names of) these angels on a copper *lamella* and conceal it in the east, so it will be exposed to the sun at sunrise.[46]   Do everything in purity and you will succeed.

---

[45] For the tenth angel read אל צדק as one word with Ms. ח.

[46] Literally, "at its arising."

Upon the eleventh step stand these:

155 RPDY'L   DMW'L   M'RYNWS   'MYN'L

     SHY'L   ᶜQRY'L   'DNY'L   RDQY'L

     ŚLMY'L   'STTY'L   ST'L   'GLGLTWN

     'RMWT   PRHG'L   NPPMYWT

These, their position is upon the eleventh step. There
is fear where they stand, a great multitude stationing
(themselves) and establishing camps of ministering (angels) in
the heaven, for on their command angels of fire run and return,
causing (men) to descend from greatness and rise to splendor.
160 They fly to and fro, resuming their places, glorifying their
creator and extolling their maker.

If you wish to restore to office one who has fallen from
his place, a king, or minister, or governor, or judge, take oil
and honey and fine flour and place them in a new glass vial,[47]
and purify yourself from all impurity, and do not eat *nevelah*[48]
and do not touch a woman's bed,[49] for seven days. Then on the
seventh day stand beneath the moon, in its fourteenth, fif-
165 teenth, or sixteenth day,[50] and take the vial in your hand, and
write on it (the names of the angels of) this encampment of the

---

[47]פיאלי for φιάλη.

[48]That is meat from an animal which has died from natural causes.

[49]This expression should probably be understood as a metaphoric
prohibition of cohabitation, though the literal meaning may be
understood as a Rabbinic precaution against impurity.

[50]That is, "on the full moon." It seems to be implied by 2:163
that one may begin preparations on either the seventh, eighth,
or ninth, but since 2:172 implies that the adjuration is to be
recited on all three days of the full moon, one must begin
preparations on the seventh.

(eleventh) step and recite over it seven times, while facing

the moon, the names of the angels and say:

> *I bring my petition before you, O Moon, who travel*
> *by day and by night with chariots of light and angels of*
> *mercy before and behind you. I adjure you by the King*
> *who causes you to rise and set, as you are thin and*
> *become full and return to your place, so restore N son*
> *of N to his place and let him be (again) honored in*
170 *the eyes of all who see him, and as you have glory in*
> *the world, so bestow glory upon him in the eyes of all*
> *the children of Adam and Eve, and restore him to his*
> *office, and let him rule as at the beginning and let*
> *him not move from his position (again).*

Do this for him for three days, and afterwards make them[51]

into a cake and dry it at night so that the sun does not shine

on it, and have him eat it for three days, before sunrise, and

bury (the) vial, with the writing still on it,[52] in his house.

175   Upon the twelfth step stand these:

'STRYMY	BR'WT	BMR'WT	DRWDY'L
SDRLY'L	TLHBM	BRG'L	PY'L
PP'L	YKPTYNY	KLPTWN	BWBWKWK
'WMTWN	'RTMYKTWN	'SMYGDWN	SPNYG
PRNYG'L	PSYKSWK	T'GYSWN	'RTLYDY

These, their position is on the twelfth step. Surrounded

by righteousness, rays of majesty on their heads, full of

understanding, they understand how to praise (the Lord). They

180 stand in two equal companies, half of them singing and the other

half answering after them. Their language heals, their speech

binds up (wounds), and anything they mention will be successful.

---

[51] I.e., the oil, honey, and flour.

[52] Literally, "and vial bury written." One expects "and bury
the inscribed vial" in order to parallel 2:165.

If you wish to cure a headache (affecting) half the
head[53] or to bind or rebuke the spirit causing blindness, take
fat that covers the brain of a black ox, and while in (a state
of) purity, write on it the names of these angels and place it
in a silver tubular case, then bind the tube with seven colors[54]
and place it beside the pain. (In order to succeed) abstain
185   from meat, from wine, from (contact with) the dead, from
menstruating women, and from every unclean thing.

---

[53]Cf. PGM VII:199.

[54]Cf. PGM VII:271.

(THE THIRD FIRMAMENT)

The third firmament is filled with storerooms of mist from which the winds go forth, and inside it are encampments of thunder from which lightning emanates. Within, three princes sit on their thrones; they and their raiment have an appearance like fire and the appearance of their thrones is like fire, fire that gleams like gold, for they rule over all the angels of fire. They are like fire in their strength and their voices are like the roar of a peal of thunder. And their eyes are like sunbeams, and they rule over the wheels of flame and fire. Moreover, they have wings to fly. The whinnying of their mouths is as horses,[1] their appearance like torches; when they speak they cause trembling, when they shout they cause weakness. They soar in every direction and fly to every corner (of the world).

These are the names of the princes who rule in the habitation[2] which is the third firmament. The name of the first is YBNY'L, the name of the second is RHTY'L, and the name of the third is DLQY'L. YBNY'L is in charge of all things concerning the igniting and extinguishing of fire. RHTY'L is in charge of every chariot of fire[3] causing it to

---

[1] Cf. Nah 2:5.

[2] מעון, i.e., habitation, temple, place.

[3] The chariots of fire are the heavenly fires over which these princes rule. The circling celestial bodies are viewed as the circling chariots of the hippodrome. Thus RHTY'L appears as the ruler of chariot races and his name (RHT = run) indicates that he was created for this function. The association of RHTY'L with the other angels of fire comes through Helios who drove a fiery chariot and team and was therefore the most conspicuous of charioteers and thus became the patron of their profession.

run (successfully) or to fail.[4] DLQY'L is in charge of flames

of fire, to kindle or quench (them).

These are the names of the angels who serve YBNY'L:

ŚᶜYPY'L	'DRY'L	TDHDY'L	BᶜŚY'L
THPY'L	RLBY'L	BLNY'L	THZRY'L
'ᶜZY'L	'MNHY'L	MLTHY'L	DYBQY'L
BRŚS'L	SH'L	TTB'L	QSMY'L
TSY'L	QSTSDY'L	NMDY'L	

15

If you wish to extinguish (the fire which heats) a bath-

house so it will neither flare up nor burn, bring a salamander[5]

and place it in a glass vessel with oil aged for three years.

Do not set it upon the ground, but repeat backwards over it

seven times during the third hour of the night the name of

20   the overseer and the names of the angels who serve before him,

and say:

> *I adjure you, O salamander, in the name of YBNY'L*
> *and in the name of the angels of fire who serve him,*
> *just as you were driven from fire, so drive away and*
> *extinguish the fire from the bathhouse[6] of N son of*
> *N. And you, angels of fire, all of whose deeds pertain*
> *to fire, do not permit fire to enter or warm this*
> *bathhouse, but stand on the gates of his (the owner's)*
> *house and enter it, and make it like cold snow[7] or*
> *cold water.*

25

---

[4]Literally, "stumble." The author is writing of chariots but
thinking of horses.

[5]סלאמנדרא for σαλαμάνδρα. The salamander is well known in the
ancient world as being associated with fire. Cf. Ginzberg,
Legends 5.52, n. 157f.

[6]Deleting מהלט, i.e., "blazing" since the purpose was to prevent
ignition and the adjective implies the bathhouse is already
ablaze.

[7]Cf. Prov 25:13.

Then take the flask of oil and put some of it on the four

corners of each and every room. If you wish to undo the spell,

take some of the remaining oil and stand facing the sun and

repeat the name of YBNY'L and the names of the angels who serve

him and say:

> *I adjure you, angel of fire and angel of conflagra-*
> *tion, that you will undo what I have bound and will*
> *permit the angels standing at the gates of the bathhouse*
> *of N son of N to ignite and kindle its fire as before.*

30

Then take the flask of oil and pour (some of it) in the

four corners of each room and the fire will ignite and burn.

These are the names of the angels who serve RHTY'L:

'GR'	ZRGRY	GNTS	T^CZM'
LTSRP'L	GDY'L	TMNY'L	^CQHY'L
GWHPNY'L	'RQNY	SPYQW'L	MWŚY'L
SWSY'L	HTNY'L	ZKRY'L	'KNSP
SDQY	'HSP	NKMR'	PRDY'L
QLYLY'L	DRWMY'L		

35

8

8These characters are from Ms. ח . Cf. Second Firmament,
note 14 (p.46).

If you wish to race horses, (even) when they are exhausted,
so that they will not stumble in their running, that they will
be swift as the wind, and the foot of no living thing will pass
them, and they will win popularity in their running, take a
silver *lamella* and write upon it the names of the horses and
the names of the angels and the name of the prince[9] who is
over them and say:

*I adjure you angels of running, who run amid
the stars, that you will gird with strength and
courage the horses that N is racing and his charioteer[10]
who is racing them. Let them run and not become weary
nor stumble. Let them run and be swift as an eagle.
Let no animals stand before them,[11] and let no other
magic or witchcraft affect them.*

Take the *lamella* and conceal it in the racing lane (of
the one) you wish to win.

These are the names of the angels who serve DLQY'L:

NWRY'L	'ZLYBN	'YLY'L	MLKYH
HYLY'L	HRH'L	SLQY'L	SGRY'L
PSKY'L	CQRY'L	SMNY'L	SBBY'L
NHLY'L	TGMLY'L	'MYNW'L	TLBCP
QTHNY'L	'PRY'L	'NGY'L	MSRY'L
'MNGN'N			

If you wish to give proof[12] (of your powers) to your

---

[9]The texts read "princes," but the singular is necessary.
Cf. Ms. ‎ח

[10]‎הניוכוס for ἡνίοχος.

[11]Cf. Dan 8:4.

[12]‎דוקמי probably for δοκιμή - "proof" or "demonstration,"
but possibly δόγμα - i.e. "example." Cf. Second Firmament.
note 33 (p.51).

beloved or to your friend, for example, to fill a house with

fire which will not burn, take a root[13] of a wild plant[14] and

put it on burning coals and as the smoke rises in the house,

50   recite the names of the angels and the name of their overseer,

who is DLQY'L. When the smoke rises seven times, and when the

smoke will be....[15] all those who see it will see it as fire.

When you recite the names of the angels say:

> *I adjure you, O angels cloaked in fire, by Him*
> *who is all fire, who sits upon a throne of fire, and*
> *whose ministers are a flaming fire,[16] and encampments*
> *of fire serve before Him. By His great name I adjure*
55   > *you, that you show me this great miracle and fill*
> *this house with your fire. Let me and all with me*
> *see this great miracle and not be afraid.*

When you finish your words, you will see the house filled

with fire. If you wish to cause (the fire) to subside speak

the adjuration backwards and say:

> *Angels of fire, extinguish, extinguish at once,*
> *hurry, make haste.*[17]

How great are your works O Lord, you have made all of

them in wisdom.[18]

---

[13]Reading עקד for עגר.

[14]אגריאופורים for ἀγρίοφορος.

[15]The text seems corrupt. We seem led to understand, "and when
the smoke will be (all that can be seen) all those who see it
will see it as fire."

[16]Cf. Ps 104:4

[17]Cf. 1 Sam 20:38

[18]Cf. Ps 104:24. This is the end of the Third Firmament and not
part of the adjuration.

(THE FOURTH FIRMAMENT)

The fourth firmament is pitched[1] upon a storm wind, and stands on pillars of fire, and is held up by crowns of flame,[2] and full of treasuries of strength, also storehouses of dew. As each of its corners are swift angels running with each other, prancing, prancing.[3]

Within are seven rivers of fire and water, and along them, on both sides, stand innumerable angels. On one side stand

5   angels of fire that burn with an incandescent flame and on the other side angels of cold wrapped in hailstones. Neither do the (angels of cold) quench (the angels of fire) nor do (the angels of fire) ignite the (angels of cold). These immerse themselves in the rivers of fire and those immerse themselves in the rivers of water,[4] and they all recite and chant[5] songs and praises to the Life of the World for He created them to glorify His power.

Within the (fourth) firmament is the lovely bridal chamber of the sun, filled with light and all aflame. The angels of fire, girded with strength, surround him (the sun) and lead him

10   during the day. Then the angels of water, their bodies like

---

[1]That is, it is pitched like a tent upon its posts.

[2]Greek capitals on columns seem implied.

[3]Cf. Judg 5:22 .

[4]The immersion is for ritual purification. Presumably they immerse themselves in the river of their own substance, rather than the opposite, but the text leaves the question open.

[5]They thus alternate like a choir. The singing thus seems to be antiphonal.

67

the sea and their voices like the voice of waters[6] strengthen themselves with an adornment of might and lead him at night.

These are the names of the angels that lead him during the day:

'BR'SKS	MRMR'WT	MWKTY'L	M'RYT
ṢDQY'L	YḤSY	ḤSY'L	RB'L
Y'BWK	MY'L	KRYMK'	MRM'N
PW'L	GBRY'L	'ŚTWN	TWQPY'L
'LY'L	NPLY	'W'L	QWDŚY'L
HWDY'L	NRWMY'L	YRŚY'L	MLKY'L
'GRYT'L	LHGY'L	MNWRY'L	PL'W'L
NWRY'L	HRM'Y'L	NSBRY'L	

These are the princes of the encampments who lead the sun during the day.[7]

And these are the names of the angels who lead him at night:

PRSY'L	ṢRṢY'L	^{c}GY'L	NBYM'L
^{c}MY'L	YSRY'L	'SM^{c}W'L	ŚPṬY'L
Ś'W'L	RDRY'L	Ś^{c}SY'L	LYBB'L
BNRY'L	ṢGRY'L	MNH'L	LMY'L
PRY'L	PDH'L	LYBR'L	RBṢ'L
ḤMQY'L	BGHY'L	NBRY'L	QṢPY'L
R^{c}DNY'L	ḤTNY'L	'SPPY'L	ḤLW'L
ŚM'Y'L	ZḤZḤ'L	NKBRY'L	PṢ'L
QMNY'L	ZH'L	ḤDY'L	

---

[6]Perhaps read כקול מים רבים, "like the voice of many waters." Cf. Ps 93:4.

[7]Apparently each of the thirty-one named here and below is a leader of others. Note the first angel, ἅβρασαξ, is a transliteration of the correct spelling.

These are the princes of the encampments who lead him at night.

25   If you wish to view the sun during the day, seated in his
chariot and ascending; guard yourself, take care, and keep pure
for seven days from all (impure) food, from all (impure) drink,
and from every unclean thing.[8] Then on the seventh day stand
facing (the sun) when he rises and burn incense of spices
weighing three shekels before him, and invoke seven times the
names of the angels that lead him during the day. Then if you
30   are not answered after these seven times, go and invoke them in
reverse order seven times, and say:

> I adjure you, angels that lead the sun in the
> power of your strength on the heavenly paths to
> illuminate the world, by the One whose voice shakes
> the earth, who moves mountains in His anger, who
> calms the sea with His power, who shakes the pillars
> of the world with His glance, who sustains every-
> thing with His arm, who is hidden form the eyes of
> all the living, who sits upon the throne of greatness
> of the kingdom of the glory of His holiness, and
35 > who moves through the entire world; I repeat (your
> names) and adjure you by His great, fearful, powerful,
> majestic, forceful, mighty, holy, strong, wondrous,
> secret, exalted, and glorious name;[9] that you will
> do my will and desire at this time and season, and
> will remove the radiance of the sun[10] so I may see
> him face to face as he is in his bridal chamber.
> Let me not catch fire from your fire and give me[11]
> permission to do my will.

---

[8]Abstinence from impure food and drink seems implied rather
than a fast. This creates a parallel to "unclean things" and
follows the same pattern as previous commands of abstinence
found in SHR.

[9]For an example of this type of listing see BT Berakhot 33b.

[10]The rays of the sun obscure the sun angel.

[11]Reading יל for לו with Ms. ל .

At the completion of your adjuration, you will see him

in his bridal chamber and you can ask him (to foretell

40   questions) of death or life, good or evil. And if you wish to

release him, repeat the adjuration and say:

> *I adjure you that you return the radiance of the*
> *sun to its place as in the beginning.*

Then the sun will go on his way.

If you wish to see the sun during the night, proceeding

(on his course) in the north,[12] purify (yourself) for three

weeks of days from all (impure) food and drink, and from every

45   unclean thing. Then stand during the third hour[13] in the

night watches, wrapped in white garments, and say twenty-one

times[14] the name of the sun and the names of the angels that

lead him at night, and then say:

> *I adjure you, angels that fly through the air of*
> *the firmament, by the One who sees but is not seen, by*
> *the King who uncovers all hidden things and sees all*
> *secret things, by the God who knows what is in darkness,*
50 > *and who transforms the shadows into morning,[15] and who*
> *illumines the night as the day, before whom all secrets*
> *are as clear as the sun, for whom there is nothing too*
> *difficult.[16] In the name of the Holy King who walks*
> *upon the wings of the wind,[17] by the letters of the*
> *complete name that was revealed to Adam in the Garden*
> *of Eden, (by)[18] the Ruler of the planets,[19] and the*

---

[12]Cf. 1 Enoch 72:5.

[13]Cf. PGM XXXVI:136.

[14]This adjuration is triple the previous one in both number of
days and times the adjuration is spoken.

[15]Cf. Amos 5:8.

[16]Cf. Jer 32:17.

[17]Cf. Ps 104:3.

[18]Reading במושל for המושל .

[19]"By the ruler of the planets," stars or fate.

sun, and the moon, who[20] bow down before Him as
slaves before their masters, by the name of the
wondrous God, I adjure you, that you will make
known to me this great miracle that I desire, and
that I may see the sun in his power in the (celestial)
55   *circle (traversed by) his chariot, and let no hidden*
thing be too difficult for me. Let me see him per-
fectly today, and let me ask him what I wish, and
let him speak with me as a man speaks with his friend
and tell me the secret of the depths, and make known
to me hidden things, and let no evil thing happen
to me.

When you finish speaking, you will hear a peal of thunder

from the north and you will see something like lightning come

forth and light up the earth before you. And after you see him,

you will assuredly bow down to the ground and fall upon your

60   face to the earth and pray this prayer:

Holy Helios who rises in the east, good mariner,
trustworthy leader of the sun's rays, reliable
(witness), who of old didst establish the mighty
wheel (of the heavens), holy orderer, ruler of the
axis (of the heaven), Lord, Brilliant Leader, King,
Soldier.[21]   I, N son of N, present my supplication
before you, that you will appear to me without
65   *(causing me) fear, and you will be revealed to*
me without causing me terror, and you will conceal
nothing from me and will tell me truthfully all that
I desire.

---

[20]Reading המשתחוים for משתחוים.

[21]The prayer to Helios here is transliterated into Hebrew from
Greek. Cf. Margalioth, Sepher 12 and 99f. The following
transcription differs from Margalioth in the underlined words:
εὐσεβὴς ἀνατολικὸν Ἥλιος, ναύτης, ἀγαθός, πιστὸς
ἀκτῶν κορυφαῖος,

εὔπιστος, ὅς πάλαι τροχὸν ὄβριμον καθίστης, κοσμητὴς
ἅγιος.

πολοκράτωρ, κύριε, πομπός εὔφωτος, τύραννος,
στρατιώτης.

Then stand up and you will see (the sun) in the north
proceeding to the east.[22] After this, put your hands behind
you, and bow your head low, and ask whatever you desire. And
after you have questioned him, lift your eyes toward heaven
and say:

> *'WRPLY'L, 'WRPLY'L,*[23] *I adjure you by the One who
> formed you, for His splendor and His glory, to illumi-
> nate His world, and who gave you rulership of the day,
> that you will not harm me,*[24] *and will not terrify me.
> I shall neither fear nor tremble, and you will return
> to your course in peace when I release you*[25] *and you
> will not pause in your course from now on forever.*[26]

> AMEN SELAH.[27]

70

---

[22] Cf. 1 Enoch 72:5.

[23] אורפליאל, this is apparently a name for the sun. Possibly
אור פלי אל. The "marvelous" or "hidden" "light of God."
Where פלי = פלאו פלאיה

[24] Cf. PGM I:346; IV:3122; V:41.

[25] Reading ואתירך for וחתירך.

[26] Cf. Ps 115:18.

[27] This is the conclusion of the Fourth Firmament and not
part of the preceeding adjuration.

(THE FIFTH FIRMAMENT)

The fifth firmament is exceedingly exalted. It is
magnificent in appearance, for within it are clouds of splendor.
It is filled with angels of majesty, and within it (their knees)
knock with fear. They are stationed in troop after troop,
glorifying (the One) who carved them into flame. The sound of
their running is like the crashing of the sea, and their walk is
like wheels of thunder. Therein, moreover, are twelve princes
of glory seated upon magnificent thrones, the appearance of their

5   thrones is like that of fire. They quarter the heavens at the
middle by facing the four directions of the world, three by
three toward each direction.[1] And (the) angels run when they
send them, and their roaring shakes the world. Lightnings issue
from their breath and they have wings of fire and are wreathed
with crowns of fire, and the (fifth) firmament shines from the
lustre of their faces. They are in charge of the twelve months
of the year and understand what will be in each and every month,
and without them nothing can happen, for they were created for

10   this. Each is stationed over his month[2] since they make known
month by month that which will be in each and every year.

These are the names of the twelve princes of glory of the
fifth firmament:

Ṡ^CPY'L	DGHY'L	DYDN'WR	T^CNBWN
TRWRGR	MWR'L	PHDRWN	YLDNG
'NDGNWR	MPNY'L	HṠNDRNWS	'BRKY'L

---

[1] This seems slightly redundant. Perhaps one ג should be deleted,
thus reading "three toward each direction.

[2] Cf. Isa 47:13.

These are they who are in charge of the twelve months of the
year, from the month of Nisan to the month of Adar, each in
his month, as they are written.[3]

15   If you wish to know in which month you will be taken from
the world, or what will occur in each and every month, or in
which month there will be rain, whether the grain will be
plentiful, whether the olive tree will drop its fruit, or in
which month kings will set forth for war, or in which month
there will be pestilence among men and cattle, or in which
month an epidemic will fall among men, or whatever you wish
(to know); ask them and you will know.

        If you wish to know in which month you will be taken from
20   the world;[4] take refined gold *lamellae* and make from them twelve
pieces of foil,[5] then write on each of them the name of an angel
and the name of his month. Then take good oil that has aged for
seven years and throw all the pieces of foil into it and recite
this adjuration seven times over the oil, and say:

>   *I adjure you, O angels of wisdom and understanding,*
> *by the One who spoke and the world came into being, by*
> *the name of the God of Truth, the majestic and glorious,*
25 *The King high and exalted, strong and powerful, mighty*
> *and wondrous, God of all creatures, Refuge of Hosts,*
> *righteous, pure and upright and trustworthy, and by*
> *the name (of Him) who established you over all the*
> *months of the year, He who sits in hidden heights,[6] who*

---

[3]This probably means "as they are written above," i.e., the
preceeding list gives them in the order of their months from
Nisan to Adar.

[4]Cf. PGM I:188; XIII:711.

[5]Literally, "hammered out pieces."

[6]Cf. Ps 91:1.

*reveals secret mysteries, who rules over death and
life, who is King forever and ever and ever, who is
established for all eternity. By this adjuration,
the great, powerful, strong, fearful, terrible,
wondrous, pure, and holy, I adjure you that you will*
30   *truthfully make known to me the month in which I
will be taken, and tell me my fate,[7] in accordance
to my request.*

Then put the oil in a new glass vessel (and place it) under

the stars for seven nights without exposing it to the sun. And

on the seventh night, get up in the middle of the night, and

look at the oil and see which month is written upon whichever

piece of foil floats on the surface of the oil. In that month

it is your fate to be taken. But before you perform this rite,

35   purify yourself from all impurity for three weeks of days, and

guard yourself from all (meat of) small animals[8] and from all

that yields blood (when slaughtered) even fish, and do not

drink wine, and do not come near a woman, and do not touch a

grave, be wary of nocturnal pollution, and walk in humility and

prayer, and make your prayers and supplications long, and devote

your heart to the fear of heaven, and you will succeed.

After the rite, take the oil and be careful of it for it

has great healing power. Make a ring of purified silver, with

a large hollow space within.[9] Take all the pieces of foil and

---

[7]Literally, "cast my lot for me."

[8]See 1:223; 2:8; and note 71, First Firmament (p.41); note 6,
Second Firmament (p.43).

[9]מגלקמוס   perhaps for μεγαλοκοιλος i.e. "pot bellied."
The equivalent is dubious, but the sense is clear: a ring with
a large top containing a compartment for storage.

40   and put them in the ring with a white flower[10] and with

asbestos,[11] and seal (it) and place it on your finger; then

no evil eye and no evil spirit will come near you, and no evil

thing will have dominion in (your) house. In the oil is a

great (power of) healing to the sick.

---

[10] פרח לבן   is literally "white flower," and is possibly Greek
in origin. Cf. PGM XII:356. Possibly an extract or wine made
from the flower.

[11] אמיינטון   for ἀμίαντος . Cf. 2:101 and note 36,
Second Firmament (p.52).

(THE SIXTH FIRMAMENT)

As for the sixth firmament, its storehouses are full of honey.[1] Within is the place prepared for the spirits of the righteous. Light and fire encompass it and within are myriads, thousands upon thousands,[2] and armies and encampments (of angels) standing in awe and trembling. And on the head of each of them is (what) appears as a crown of fire, and their fire has the appearance of gold. The regiments of the army march within (the sixth firmament), and their strength is like an

5   inextinguishable fire and they are in fear from dread of their rulers. For two officers rule over them, one in the west of the (sixth) firmament and one in the east. And before the armies of spirits are myriads of angels created from flame and burning like fire. Their bodies are like fiery coals and upon coals of fire is their station. And they tremble and shake to sing forth[3] songs and praises to the Exalted One of the Universe, who has prepared them to praise His honor and honor His praise.

10   These are the holy angels who rule over all the encampments of the sixth firmament. The name of the first is 'PRKSY[4] and the name of the second is TWQPYRS. And all the princes of the encampments serve before them.

---

[1] נופת, or possibly "fine flour."

[2] Cf. Ps 68:18.

[3] Deleting עמהם, "with them," following Ms. ר.

[4] ἀβραξας ? The common ancient spelling was ἀβρασαξ. Cf. 4:14 and Fourth Firmament, note 7 (p.68).

77

These are the heads of the encampments which are in the
west of the firmament:

WYWTN	DWKMS'L	KRH'L	'ṢRY'L
BYW'L	NRH'L	GSQY'L	GR^{C}YH
ṢRY'L	MSGY'L	HNY'L	'WRPNY'L
'QWDW	MWK'L	'LNYTK'L	DM'L
'KZ'N	ṢYR'YWM	NHRY'L	BHDRK
ṢWPRY'L	SDRKYN	DBWB'WR	'MLY'L
TMPNYH	BHHML	PRNYN	'MSTY'L
TYMNHRQ			

Over these 'PRKSY, who has his camp in the west, is ruler.

These are the heads of the encampments which are in the
east of the firmament:

GWRY'L	SNY'L	^{C}ZRY'L	ṢRY'L
'LY'L	MLKY'L	MLMY'L	SMY'L
RNHY'L	'QRY'L	QṢTY'L	'BRKY'L
ṢDRY'L	SPYPY'L	'RM'T	DMW'L
MRY'L	^{C}NNY'L	NYPLY'L	DRMY'L
G^{C}ṢY'L	MNHR'L	BHNYRY'L	'PṢRY'L
QL^{C}Y'L	HDRNY'L	DLRY'L	Ṣ^{C}PY'L
DLGLY'L	^{C}DNNY'L	THRY'L	DBRY'L
HMNKY'L	HNY'L	TWBY'L	

Over these TWQPYRS, who has his camp in the east of the
firmament is ruler.

If you wish to go on a journey (or) to war[5] and if you
wish to return (safely) from the war or from the journey, or

---

[5]Reading למלחמה או for למלחמה, to correspond to the clear
separation following "to return from the war or from the journey."

(if you wish) to flee from the city and you want it to appear

that a large and powerful company is with you, so that all who

see you will be afraid of you, as of one who has with him a

military escort armed[6] with swords and spears and all of the

implements of battle, (then) before you depart from the city or

from the place where you dwell, purify yourself from all

impurity and cleanse your flesh from all sin and transgression,

30   and make yourself an iron ring and a pure *lamella* of gold and

write (on the *lamella*) during the third day of the month,[7]

the names of the overseers and the names of the heads of the

encampments (both east and west), and put (the *lamella*) in

the ring, and engrave upon the ring, outside of the *lamella*

the image of a man and a lion.[8] Then at the time you set out

to go on your way[9] and you see that men are coming to seize

you, take the ring and put it in your mouth, and lift your eyes

to heaven with a pure and cleansed heart and repeat the names

35   of the overseers[10] and the names of the heads of the sixth

heaven who serve before them and say:

---

[6]Reading והם חגורים for ויהיו חגורי with Ms. ל .

[7]Reading בשלושה בחודש with Mss. ח and ל, thus deleting ימים.
Cf. PGM IV:170.

[8]The *lamella* is placed on the top of the ring and the engraving
is done around it.

[9]Reading בדרך instead of מן במקום שתעא למלחמה
with Mss. ת, ח, ת.

[10]'PRKSY and TWQPYRS.

*I adjure you, O angels of strength and might,[11]
by the strong and the mighty right hand (of the
Lord), by the force of His might and by the power of
His rule, by the God revealed at Mt. Sinai, by the
myriads of His chariots,[12] by the God whose ministers
are a thousand thousands of ten thousands, by the
Lord who saved Israel, all six hundred thousand,
from Egypt, by the life of the worlds, who spoke
to Moses face to face, by the Lord who brings*

40   *princes to naught,[13] by the Rock whose hand is
sufficient to save and to rescue, by the One who
commanded and ignited the camp of Sennacharib,[14] by
His name and by its letters; I repeat (your names)[15]
and adjure you that you come and stand with me, to
aid at this time in every place that I will go. Be
seen with me as a great army, in all your might and
with the strength of your spears, and let all who
see me, from near or far, and all who come to fight*

45   *me or to seize me, be shattered before me by their
great fear of your terrible appearance.[16] And let
them not be able to harm me or approach me, let fear
and terror fall upon them[17] and let fear of me fall
upon them and all the children of Adam and Eve and
upon every dangerous animal, and let them (all)
tremble and recoil from before me.*

When you finish speaking the adjuration, you will see something like fog and smoke before you. Then take the ring from
your mouth and put it on your finger. And when you come to your
house and wish to release (the angels), return the ring to your

50   mouth and stand facing the sun and repeat (the names of the)
angels in reverse order and thereafter say:

I release you, go on your way.

Then put the ring on your finger.

---

[11]Cf. Ps 24:8.

[12]Ps 68:18.

[13]Cf. Isa 40:23.

[14]Cf. 2 Kgs 19:35; and Isa 37:36. Neither source mentions any fire.

[15]I.e., those of the ministering angels and their overseers.

[16]Cf. Matt 26:53.

[17]Cf. Exod 15:16.

(THE SEVENTH FIRMAMENT)

The seventh firmament, all of it is sevenfold light, and from its light all the (seven) heavens shine. Within it is the throne of glory, set on the four glorious *Ḥayot*.[1] Also within it are the storehouses of lives,[2] and the storehouses of souls. There is no calculation or limit to the great light within it, and the fullness of the light illumines all the earth. The angels are fixed in pillars of light, and their light is as the light of the brilliant star[3] and cannot be extinguished, for their eyes are like flashes of lightning, and they stand upon the margins of (the divine) light, and glorify in fear the One who sits upon the throne of glory. For He alone sits in the heaven of His holiness, seeking out judgment, evening the scales of justice; judging in truth and speaking in righteousness.

And before Him the books of fire are open

And from before Him flow rivers of fire.[4]

When He rises[5] the gods are afraid,

And when He roars the pillars shake,

---

[1] The "living creatures" of Ezekiel's vision. Cf. Ezek 1:5ff. The *ḥayot* and *opanim* are part of or equivalent to the class of heavenly beings, like the *cherubim* in Ezek 10, who are the supports of the heavenly throne of the deity.

[2] "Lives" are here thought of as entities placed by the deity in all living things, and causing them to live. They are distinguished from "souls." Cf. Gen 2:7, "the breath of lives."

[3] This is certainly a reference to Aphrodite-Venus, who has been referred to previously. Cf. First Firmament, note 44 (p.33).

[4] Cf. Dan 7:10.

[5] Possibly "When He lifts (His voice)."

And from His voice the doorposts tremble.[6]

His soldiers stand before Him,

But they do not gaze upon His likeness.

10   For He is hidden from every eye,

And none can see Him and live.

His appearance is hidden from all,

But no appearance is hidden from Him.

He uncovers deep things from the darkness,[7]

And He knows the secrets of obscurity.

For light dwells with Him,[8]

And He puts on light as a garment.[9]

He sits on light as a throne,

And light is a wall around Him.[10]

The *Ḥayot* and *Opanim* bear Him up,

As they fly with their wings.

They have six wings each

And they cover their faces with their wings,

And they turn their faces downward.

15   Their faces are turned toward their fellows,[11]

And they do not lift their faces upwards,

Because of their fear and their terror.

---

[6] Cf. Isa 6:4.

[7] Cf. Job 12:22.

[8] Cf. Dan 2:22.

[9] Cf. Ps 102:4.

[10] Literally, "closes off what surrounds Him."

[11] Literally, "to the four of them."

Troops upon troops stand one above another before Him,

And immerse themselves in rivers of purity.

And wrap themselves in garments of white fire,

And sing with humility in a strong voice:

"Holy Holy Holy is the Lord of Hosts,

The whole world is full of His glory,[12]

He is prior to all creatures;

He was when earth and heaven were not yet.

He is alone;

There is no stranger with Him.

By His strength He upholds the heaven(s),

And in all the heavens He is feared,

20   And by all the angels He is revered,

For by the breath of His mouth they were formed

And to glorify His power they were established.

He (acts) alone and who can turn Him back?[13]

And if He commands none can annul.

For He is the King of Kings of Kings,

Ruling over all of the kings of the earth,

And exalted among the angels of heaven.

He searches hearts before they are formed,

And He knows thoughts before they occur.

Blessed be His name

And blessed the greatness of His glory.

---

[12]Cf. Isa 6:3.

[13]Cf. Job 23:13.

For ages and ages,

And for an eternity of eternities.

For there is no God apart from Him,[14]

5   And there is no God beside Him.

Blessed is His name in each generation

And blessed in the heavens on high.

Blessed is His name with its might,

And blessed its mention with the beauty of His power.

For as His name so is His praise as it has been said (in

scripture): As is your name, O God, so is your praise to

the ends of the earth; your right hand is full of

righteousness.[15]

He brings the pure to reverence Him,[16]

And in His wrath drives away the impure.

He moves mountains by His might and strength,

They did not know when He overturned them in His wrath.[17]

He holds the world as a cluster of grapes,

30   Bearing all that was, is, and will be.[18]

He is the Ancient of Days,[19]

---

[14]Cf. 2 Sam 22:32.

[15]This is a prose gloss which breaks the continuity of the hymn.

[16]Literally, "to His fear," i.e., to worship and magical practices.

[17]Cf. Job 9:5.

[18]Cf. Heb 1:3.

[19]Cf. Dan 7:9.

And with Him are enduring riches and righteousness.[20]

Blessed be His glory from His habitation,

And blessed (be He) in the beauty of His dignity.

The hearts of those who fear Him He fills with knowledge,

To search and to know the power of the fear of His name.

Blessed be His name in the dwelling place of His splendor,

And blessed in the beauty of His strength.

Blessed be His name in the storehouses of snow,

And blessed in the rivers of flames.

Blessed be His name in the mists of brilliance,

And blessed in the clouds of glory.

35   Blessed be His name in the myriads of chariots,[21]

And blessed in the thousands upon thousands (of His

warriors).

Blessed be His name in the chains of fire,

And blessed in the ropes of flame.

Blessed be His name in the peals of thunder,

And blessed in the bolts of lightning.

Blessed be His name in the mouths of all on earth,

And blessed in the depths of the earth.

Blessed be His name amid all the deserts,

And blessed amid the waves of the sea.

Blessed be His name alone on His throne,

---

[20] Cf. Prov 8:18.

[21] Cf. Ps 68:18.

And blessed in dwelling places of His majesty,

Blessed be His name in the mouth of all living,

And blessed in the song of every creature.

40   Blessed be the Lord forever,

AMEN, AMEN, HALLELUJAH.

APPENDIX: ANGELIC LISTS

THE FIRST FIRMAMENT

And these are the names of the angels of the first encampment who
serve אורפניאל:

בומדי דמנא אנוך אלפי אמוך קטיביא קטרופי גמהי פאאור נרנתק
רקהוני אורנה מאות פרוכה אקילאה תרקויה ברוק סחרורא אתגני
גילאן תכת ארנוב אשמי יוצש כפון כרבי גירשום פריאן ששמע
אבבא נתנאל אראל אניף תרואור עבדיאל יוום אלון מואל ללף
יחספת רחגל רומאפי יכוני ארניאל פובנן כדיאל זכריאל אגדלן
מיגאל גאופר כרתה כילדה דיגל אלנו תירלי סבלה אביאל אל
כסיל סיקמה אשבה יותנה ראלכה חליאן אפתיאל תיאמיאל אלאל
נוניאל אפיכה תלגיאל נענה אסתיאל.

These are the names of the angels of the second encampment who
serve תיגרה:

אכסתר מרסום ברכיב כמשו אשטיב כריתאל אדיר גבא אקרבא
אנבור כביר תילה בריתור תרטם נטפיאל פריאל תרוחון שלהבין
אשלבא משתוב גרחתא חגרא איטמיאל חגל לגח מניתיאל תנימיאל
איכרית אבריתא רכילאל חשתך pprש אסתרוף אודיאל אשביר
מלכיאל ארוש דשוא המך תרגח זמבות הצניפלפת שווא אשפור
ארק קנומיאל נהיאל גדיאל אדק ימומיאל פרוג דחגיאל דגריאל
אגריאל ארונור דונרניא דלכת תבל תליאל אליאל מותאר אלפיאל
פיתפרא לפוס אור טמר אדליאל אסטורין אזותי איסטורטי דאוברת
ברגמי דמומיאל דיגרא אביבאל פרוטיאל קומיאל דגוגרא דלגיאל
פדותיאל.

These are the names of the angels who serve דנהל in the third
encampment:

אוגרבבו אובשאל ברתוביאל כלוביאל רחביאל אוהיאל כרבתון
כרבא דאינוט איניך אבירס אתגלא אותות אשתנואל אשפר תגריאל
אמיכאל אתדשו אוריאל ארמוד אסחון אכאל אנאור אסכירא
לביאל אלעשה חסניאל למושי אדות תירום אלפי אימיך ארגלא
מיגאל אליאל מדניאל.

These are the names of the angels who serve כלמייה in the fourth
encampment:

אבריה אימרהי דמנאי אמנאי אמנהר יאמנוך פטכיא טוביאל גוליאל אופרי
גמהי אורניאל פרייכיהו יארן לטמיאל אוריט תימוגו אנמרי
אלמיניאל יכמטו סטרטו צבעקני בורתיאס רספות כרסון אמאף
ופאטנא אחאל סאביאל בלקיר פכהור הסתר סתריאל אליסס חלסיאל
טרספו קרסטוס מלכיאל ארדק חסדיאל אחסף אמיאל פרנוס
גדיאל סביבאל.

These are the angels who serve אסימור in the fifth encampment:

בתואר שכינתתך אדומא תקו מקפא להבא עלי עזי שכניאל כנור
בנש קרבא סרך חלשיאל הרמנע עבר הוד מלכיה פרעתוף אדעת
קוף מנגמלך דינמור אלפנטוס דידריוך כלנה נינחיא דצנחיא מלגדם
דימהן ליברנך תתקהה אפניאל זביטור דכנסור רמגדל להתקוף

עלי גדגדל פרוץ מסרוץ כדיר מוס דיקנא נשר תוב דרומיאל
דיראז דמולא דידיאל טעי כרם אתר עקב הונמורא אנקיו גזריאל
צביאל צביודע ייקר אדות רגביאל.

These are the names of the angels who serve פסכר in the sixth
encampment:

אזיאל ארביאל טריפון פוכבוס פסתמר לינניאל קרונידן שוכדון
סלבידם עמיאל עוזיאל פניאל תרמיאל חממיאל צרמיאל נימומס
נודנייא בארריבא זוננום חסטואל סדריאל הופניאון קדמיאל כפנייא
ארמיאל עדמון הרמור צפליאל ספריאל קחניאל שבכרייא ארמוניס
טופומוס פצציאל חטפיאל פרסומון נחליאל.

These are the names of the angels who serve בואל in the seventh
encampment:

נוהריאל דבבאל דימתמר דבאל מחשיו אאור דיאם בביתאל סרורא
אהגייה פרופיאל מכסיאל עלזיאל תכורכס קרומיאל רמיאל לחסון
סלחיאל אחיאל אכר אובר סרוגיאל ידואל שמשיאל שפטיאל
רחביא אחמודא מרמרין אנוך אלפרט אומיגרא קרוכנס סרפיאל
גדריאל ארדודא פורטניאל אגמיאל רהטיאל דיתרון חזאל פתואל
גלגלא דמנצר זזיאל.

THE SECOND FIRMAMENT

Upon the first step stand these:
אחמריאל הדריאל רציאל הסעיאל דמימיאל זבדיאל רנזיאל
ענשאל כטבראל.

Upon the second step stand these:
עזזיאל חננאל פצציאל ישעיאל דלקיאל ארפדא מראות ריפיפיס
אמניאל נחמיאל פזירום ענבאל.

Upon the third step stand these:
יהואל דעיהו אליאל ברכיאל עלי ספום פנימור אלעזר גבליאל
כמשיאל אודהאל יעצאל רפפיאל פספיאל.

Upon the fourth step stand these:
צגריאל מלכיאל אונביב פגריאל ענניאל כלנמייא אומיאל מפנור
כוזזיבא אלפיאל פריביאל צעקמיה כדומיאל אשמדע הודיה יחזיאל.

Upon the fifth step stand these:
קונאקריאל פתוניאל נקריאל איאל יאבותיאו בבסבאו בכפי מבום
סכתבאו אמריאל יאלאל מכסאבו.

Upon the sixth step stand these:
אביהוד קיטר זלקיאל סתריאל אדרך גחליאל תמכיאל סמכיה רבעיאל
יונקמיאל שמיהוד מהריאל גומיאל כרכוס קנז קניאל כנטון.

Upon the seventh step stand these:
פתחיה רזיאל אגריאל הגדיאב אדרון כרקטא קטיפור אבריאל
שתקיאל עמיאל סיכברדום.

Upon the eighth step stand these:
אברה ברקיאל אדוניאל עזריאל ברכיאל עמיאל קדשיאל מרגיאל
פרואל פניאל מרבניאל מרניסאל שמיאל עמניאל מתנאל הוד הוד.

Upon the ninth step stand these:
גדודיאל סכסיאל תרסוניאל נצחיאל אצדא רבניא חלילאל תוקפיאל
סמכיאל פדהאל קרבא ציאל פראל פתחיאל.

Upon the tenth step stand these:
דכריאל חריאל שבקיאל אתכיאל סמיכאל מרמואל קנאל צפתף יהאך
אל צדק אכפף עזמאל מכמיכאל תרכיאל תבגיאל.

Upon the eleventh step stand these:
רפדיאל דמואל מארינוס אמינאל צחיאל עקריאל אדניאל רדקיאל
שלמיאל אסתטיאל סטאל אגלגלתון ארמות פרחגאל נפפמיות.

Upon the twelfth step stand these:
אסטרימי בראות במראות דרודיאל שדרליאל תלהבם ברגאל פיאל
פפאל יכפתיני כלפתון בובוכוך אומטון ארטמיכטון אשמיגדון
ספניג פרניגאל פסיכסוך תאגישון ארטלידי.

THE THIRD FIRMAMENT

These are the names of the angels who serve יבניאל:
שעיפיאל אדריאל תדהדיאל בעשיאל טהפיאל רלביאל בלניאל
תחזריאל אעזיאל אמנחאל מלתיחיאל דיבקיאל ברשסאל סחאל
תתבאל קסמיאל טסיאל קסטסדיאל נמדיאל.

These are the names of the angels who serve רהטיאל:
אגרא זרגרי גנטס תעזמא לתסרפאל גדיאל תמניאל עקהיאל
גוחפניאל ארקני צפיקואל מושיאל סוסיאל התניאל זכריאל
אכנסף צדקי אחסף נכמרא פרדיאל קליליאל דרומיאל.

These are the names of the angels who serve דלקיאל:
נוריאל אזליבן איליאל מלכיה חיליאל חרהאל שלקיאל צגריאל
פסכיאל עקריאל סמניאל צבביאל נחליאל תגמליאל אמינואל תלבעף
קטחניאל אפריאל אנגיאל משריאל אמנגנאן.

THE FOURTH FIRMAMENT

These are the names of the angels that lead (the sun) during the day:

אבראסכס מרמראות מוכתיאל מארית צדקיאל יחסי חסיאל רבאל
יאבוך מיאל כרימכא מרמאן פואל גבריאל אשתון תוקפיאל אליאל
נפלי אואל קודשיאל הודיאל נרומיאל ירשיאל מלכיאל אגריתאל
להגיאל מנוריאל פלאואל נוריאל הרמאיאל נסבריאל.

And these are the names of the angels that lead (the sun) during the night:

פרסיאל צרציאל עגיאל נבימאל עמיאל ישריאל אשמעואל
שפטיאל שאואל רדריאל שעסיאל ליבבאל בנריאל צגריאל מנהאל
למיאל פריאל פדהאל ליבראל רבצאל חמקיאל בגהיאל נבריאל
קצפיאל רעדניאל חתניאל אספפיאל חלואל שמאיאל זחזחאל
נכבריאל פצאל קמניאל זהאל חדיאל.

THE FIFTH FIRMAMENT

These are the names of the twelve princes of glory of the fifth firmament:

שעפיאל דגהיאל דידנאור תענבון תרורגר מוראל
פחדרון ילדנג אנדגמור מפניאל חשנדרנוס אברכיאל.

THE SIXTH FIRMAMENT

These are the heads of the encampments which are in the west of the firmament:

ויותן דוכמסאל כרהאל אשריאל ביואל נרהאל גצקיאל גרעיה
שריאל מסגיאל חניאל אורפניאל אקודו מוכאל אלניתכאל דמאל
אכזאן שיראיום נהריאל בהדרך שופריאל סדרכין דבובאור אמליאל
תמפניה בההמל פרנין אמצתיאל תימנהרק.

Over these אפרכסי , who has his camp in the west, is ruler.

These are the heads of the encampments which are in the east of the firmament:

גוריאל סניאל עזריאל שריאל אליאל מלכיאל מלמיאל צמיאל
רנחיאל אקריאל קשתיאל אברכיאל שדריאל ספיפיאל ארמאת דמואל
מריאל ענניאל ניפליאל דרמיאל געשיאל מנהראל בהניריאל אפשריאל
קלעיאל הדרניאל דלריאל שעפיאל דלגליאל עדנניאל טהריאל
דבריאל המנכיאל הניאל טוביאל.

Over these תוקפירס, who has his camp in the east of the firmament, is ruler.

INDICES

1. Ancient Sources

   A. Scripture

	page no.		page no.
Gen 2:7	81	Ps 24:8	80
Exod 15:16	80	68:18	77,80,
Lev 21:11	44		85
Deut 27:8	17	91:1	74
Judg 5:22	67	93:4	68
1 Sam 20:38	65	102:4	82
2 Sam 22:32	84	104:3	70
2 Kgs 19:35	80	104:4	42,65
Isa 6:3	83	104:24	65
6:4	82	107:33	42
37:36	80	115:18	72
40:12	42	Prov 8:18	85
40:23	80	25:13	62
47:13	73	Job 9:9	17
Jer 32:17	70	9:5	84
Ezek 1:4	42	12:22	82
1:5	81	23:13	83
10	81	38:35	18
18:6	43	Eccl 3:2-3	18
Amos 5:8	17, 70	Dan 2:22	82
Nah 1:4	42	7:9	84
2:5	61	7:10	81
		8:4	64
		Tob 3:7,17	48
		Matt 26:53	80
		Heb 1:3	84

   B. Magical Literature

PGM			
I:175	41	IV:345	34,37
I:188	74	IV:1034	38
I:264	55	IV:1480	34,37
I:278	30	IV:2706	46
I:346	72	IV:2891	33
		IV:2943	49
II:87	30	IV:3122	72
		IV:3210	26
III:108	42		
III:325	30	V:41	72
III:425	33	V:237	30
IV:170	79	VII:199	59
IV:222	26	VII:271	59
IV:260	30	VII:397	49

B. Magical Literature

PGM (continued)

	page no.		page no.
VII:810	46	XIII:300	52
VII:816	46	XIII:711	74
VII:860	46		
VII:915	37	XXIV:15	55
VII:922	46		
		XXXVI:136	70
XII:356	76	XXXVI:232	49
		XXXVI:370	49

DMP
22:40	37
25:27	33

C. Other Ancient Sources

	page no.
Avodah Zarah 3:1	9,53
BT Berakhot 33b	69
1 Enoch 72:5	70,72
4 Ezra 14:39	34
Josephus' Antiquities 8.2.5, #45-49	19
Liber Razielis Angeli	5
Maimonides' Mishnah Torah	53
Maseket Hekhaloth	2
Maaseh Bereshit	2
Pirke Avoth 1:1	19
Sefer Raziel	21
Shiur Komah	2
Song of Songs 1:13, Arabic tg.	33
Testament of Job 7	44

2. Non-Angelic Proper Names

	page no.		page no.
Abraham	19	Great Bear	17
Adam	17,70	Greek kings,	
Adam and Eve	34,44,45, 58,80	reckoning of	23
		Hagar	39
Amram	19	Hayot	81,82
Aphrodite-Venus	33,81	Helios	71
Ares	47	Hermes	38
Bar Cochba	48	Isaac	19
Cherubim	81	Istorgon	33
Enoch	17	Jacob	19
Enosh	17	Jared	17
Garden of Eden	70	Joshua	19

2. Non-Angelic Proper Names (continued)

	page no.		page no.
Kenan	17	Pleiades	17
Kohath	19	the Prophets	19
Lamech	17	Ram Bearer-Hermes	38
Levi	19	Sages	19
Mehallalel	17	Sennacharib	80
Methusaleh	17	Seth	17
Moses	19,80	Shamayim	21,42
Mt. Sinai	80	Shem	19
Noah	17-19	Sodom and Gomorah	28
Opanim	81,82	Solomon	19
Orion	17		

3. Names of Principal Angels

'BRKY'L	73	KWZZYB'	48
'WRPNY'L	21-24	KLMYY' (KLMY',	
'NDGNWR	73	KLMYYH)	21,32,34
'SYMWR	21,36	KRDY	27
'SMD	48	MWR'L	73
'PRKSY	77-79	MPNY'L	73
BW'L	21,40	SRWKYT	27
DGHY'L	73	ᶜWLPH	27
DYDN'WR	73	PHDRWN	73
DLQY'L	61-62,	PSKR	21,39
	64-65	QRSTWS	32,34
DNHL	21,29	RHTY'L	61,63
HHGRYT	27	RZY'L	6,17
WRPLY'L	21,23-24	SᶜPY'L	73
HSNDRNWS	73	TWQPYRS	77-79
YBNY'L	61-62	TYGRH	21,25
YLDNG	73	TᶜNBWN	73
		TRWRGR	73

4. Properties of Angels

amber	54	eyes like sunbeams	61
Ancient of Days	84	fire	21,43,45,
breath, like flaming fire	50		47,52,54,
lightning issues from	73		55,61,62,
Bridal chariot of the Sun	30,67-70		63,77
Brilliant Star, like the	81	angels of	57,65,67
bronze, helmets	50	appearance like	21
sound of	48	books of	81
chariot	55,61,69,	chains of	85
	71,80,85	cloaked in	65
charioteer	61,64	crowns of	73,77
coals, bodies like fiery	77	harnesses of	55
cold	52,67	horses of	55
dew, storehouses of	67	image of	55
directions,facing in four	73	pillars of	41,42,67

4. Properties of Angels (continued)

	page no.		page no.
fire (continued)		reed pens	56
reed pens of	56	sea, bodies like the	68
river of	50,67,81	crashing of the	73
rods of	47	sevenfold light	81
sparks of	47	snow	43
throne of	65,73	storehouses of	85
wheels of	61	spear	50,79
wings of	73	spirits, rule over	54
flame	61,67	of terror and dread	43
aflame	67	storm	48,50
created from	77	sun	30,67,69,
crowns of	67		70,72
rivers of	85	sword	55,79
ropes of	85	thrones of glory	51
fly through the air	70	thunder	47,61,85
fog	43	encampments of	61
four directions	53,73	wheels of	73
frost	43	torches	50
garments, coats of mail	50	appearance like	61
of light	82	water, angels of	67
white	70,51	voice of	68
white fire	83	weapons	
gold	61,77	bow	55
hail	43,50	brass helmet	50
hailstones	67,50	breastplate	55
wrapped in	67	coats of mail	50
honey, storehouses of	77	javelin	55
horses	55,61	shield	42,50
light	82	wheels	
pillars of	81	of flame	61
sparks of	53,67	of the heavens	71
lightning	61,85	of thunder	73
appearance of	44	winds	61, 67
swift as	48	wings of	70, 82
eyes like	81	wings	61, 82
mist	61,85	of fire	73
moisture	43		

5. Purposes Which Angels Can Be Made To Serve

to perform an act of healing	24
to afflict an enemy	26-28
to predict the future	29-31
to influence opinions in one's favor	32-35
to bind oneself to the heart of a great or wealthy woman	35
to speak with the moon or stars, question a ghost or spirit, or to make a love potion	36-39
to catch and return a fugitive	39-40
to interpret dreams	41-42
to silence enemies	44-45
to put the love of a man into the heart of a woman or arrange for a poor man to marry a rich woman	45-46

5. Purposes Which Angels Can Be Made To Serve (continued)

	page no.
to nullify evil intentions	47-48
to give an enemy insomnia	49
to light an oven in the cold	50-51
to heal a man who has had a stroke	51-52
to expel a dangerous animal or quell a rising river or sea	53
to drive away an evil spirit from a woman in childbirth	54
to protect a man going forth to battle	55
to reverse a bad court decision	56
to restore to office one who has fallen from favor	57-58
to cure a headache	58-59
to extinguish a fire in a bathhouse	62-63
to win at horse racing	64
to give proof of power by filling a house with flame which does not burn	64-65
to view the sun during the day and ask it to foretell the future	69-70
to view the sun at night and ask it questions	70-72
to know in which month one will die or what will be in each and every month	74-76
to return safely from a war or journey, to create the appearance that a mighty company is with one	78-80

6. Magical Materials

	page no.		page no.
aqueduct	49	foil (lamella)	34,74
asbestos	52,76	frankincense	24,41,51
ashes	44,45	glass cup	38
bay leaves	55	vessel	35,62,75
blood	33,34,36,	vial	26-28
	37,41,43	gold	34,54,74,
bronze			77,79
image	53	heart	33
knife	33	hieratic papyrus	29
stylus	50	honey	38,50,77
tubular case	55	image	
cake	36-38,58	of lion	79
cloak	41,47	of a man	42,53,79
coals, burning	24,41,65	ink	30
cock, white	36,37	iron	
colors, seven	59	chain	49
copper	40,45,	lamella	53
	53,56	ring	79
cup	33,38	lamella	
dog, head of a black	49	copper	40,45,53,
earthen vessel	41		56
fat	59	gold	54,75,79
flask	30,35,37,	iron	53
	38,63	lead	49
flour	36,57,77	tin	35
flower, white	76	silver	48,52,54,
			5,64

6. Magical Materials (continued)

	page no.		page no.
lead	49	sapphire stone	17
lion		silver	
blood	35	lamella	48,52,54,
cub	33		55,64
engraved	49	ring	75
heart	34	tubular case	54,59
image	79	spices	33
living water	34,36	chosen	51
musk	33	incense of	33,52,69
myrrh	24,30,33,	spikenard oil	30,31,
	41,51		50,55
myrtle, table	37	staff, marble	53
twig	38	styrax	33
oil	31,38,51,	sulphur	50,51
	55,57,62,	tin	35
	63,74,75,	tubular case	
	76	bronze	55
ox, brain of a black	59	silver	54,59
perspiration	35	water	26,28,
pottery vessels	26-27		41,42
ring	49,80	living	34,36
iron	79	wax	37,49
silver	75	wild plant, root of	65
root	65	wine	33,34,38,
salamander	62		41,43,46,
			59,75

7. Incantation Formulae

alphabets, special	46,48,	fire	65
	52,63	pillar of	41-42
animal	41,43	first hour of night	24
astrological signs	17,37,45	first year	23
backwards recitation	44,62,65,	fish	41,43,75
	69,80	food, impure	69,70
barefoot	47	fog	80
blood, guard oneself from	75	four	
brilliant star	33	corners	28,63
bread offering	44	directions	26,28,40
breath, speak under your	42	sides	54
bronze, yoke of	49	winds	18,26
city, in the midst of a	34-35	garments	28
at the entrance of	53	white	70
coal of fire	34	graves	38,75
dead, contact with	59	hands, position of	53,72
doorstep	28,35,49	head, bow the	72
drink, impure	69,70	heart	48,55
evil eye	76	house, behind a	49
face	35,38,	in a	58
	41,53	idol	44
feet, soles of	35	intercourse-	
heels of	53	cohabitation	46,56,
			57,75

7. Incantation Formulae (continued)

	page no.		page no.
iron, chains of	49	sun	30,38,51,
killed, place of the	39		56,58,80
leper	44	sunrise	58
lightning	71	Sunday	41
love potion	35	three	
meat	41,46,59,	cakes	36
	75	days	30,35,41,
nevelah	57		58
menstruating woman	43,59	hundred times	33
midnight	47	shekels	69
moon	35,36,38,	times	30,38,41,
	46,47,58		42,50
full moon	57	weeks	70,75
mouth, putting ring in	79-80	years	62
nevelah	57	years old	33
night	36,58,	tomb	38
	70,75	twenty-one times	33,34,47,70
nine days	38	twentieth of month	52
nocturnal pollution	75	twenty-ninth of month	45
north, facing	53	venereal discharge	44
palm tree, fruit of	43	wall	31
prayers	18,21,75	water	53
ritual bath	45	wind	26,38
ritual burial	31	wine, abstinence from	75
ritual purification	67	window	31
river bank	41	witchcraft	51
sea shore	41		
second hour of the night	24		
second year	23		
seven			
colors	59		
days	51,57,69		
leaves of bay tree	55		
nights	75		
pottery vessels	26		
shekels	50		
smoke rising	65		
spirits	42		
springs	26		
times	42,44,62,		
	65,69,74		
years	74		
seventh day	51,69		
seventh day of month	26		
seventh hour of day	26		
singsong whimper	39		
smoke, column of	39		
rising	65,80		
spirits	18,19,38,		
	39,42,43,		
	54,76		
stars	26,37,38		

CPSIA information can be obtained
at www.ICGtesting.com
Printed in the USA
LVOW03s1930301017

554292LV00001B/106/P